first 5

© First15

No part of this publication may be reproduced, distributed or transmitted in any form or by any means, including photocopying or electronic or mechanical method without prior written permission of the editor; except in the case of brief quotations embodied in critical reviews and certain other noncommercial uses permitted by copyright law. For permissions request, please write to us.

"Scripture quotations are from The ESV® Bible (The Holy Bible, English Standard Version®), copyright © 2001 by Crossway, a publishing ministry of Good News Publishers. Used by permission. All rights reserved."

Printed in Dallas, Texas by The Odee Company

Contact: contact@first15.org
www.first15.org

Designed by Matt Ravenelle
mattravenelle.com

ABOUT FIRST15

Spending time alone with God every day can be a struggle. We're busier – and more stressed – than ever. But still, we know it's important to spend time alone with our Creator. We know we need to read his word, pray, and worship him.

First15 bridges the gap between desire and reality, helping you establish the rhythm of meaningful, daily experiences in God's presence. First15 answers the critical questions:

- Why should I spend time alone with God?
- How do I spend time alone with God?
- How do I get the most out of my time alone with God?
- How can I become more consistent with my time alone with God?

And by answering these questions through the format of daily devotionals, you'll practice the rhythm of meeting with God while experiencing the incredible gift of his loving presence given to those who make time to meet with him.

Allow God's passionate pursuit to draw you in across the next several days. And watch as every day is better than the last as your life is built on the solid foundation of God's love through the power of consistent, meaningful time alone with him.

To learn more about First15, visit our website first15.org. First15 is available across mobile app, email, podcast, and our website. Subscribe to our devotional today and experience God in a fresh way every day.

———

ABOUT THE AUTHOR

Craig Denison is the author of First15, a daily devotional guiding over a million believers into a fresh experience with God every day. In 2015, Craig founded First15 after sensing a longing in God's heart for his people to be about relationship — real, restored relationship with him — that above all else, he simply wanted the hearts of his people. Craig began praying, dreaming, and writing. And the idea of helping people spend the first fifteen minutes of their day focusing on nothing else but growing in their relationship with God was born. The vision was birthed in Craig's heart that if we as a people would worship, read, and pray at the beginning of every day, everything could change for the better. Craig writes, speaks, and he and his wife, Rachel lead worship to help believers establish a more tangible, meaningful connection with God.

———

CONTENTS

Faith
Week 1

The marks of a true Christian
Week 2

Encountering God
Week 3

God's heart to meet with man
Week 4

Day 1 – At the Heart of Faith — 12-15
Day 2 – Faith Comes by Hearing — 16-19
Day 3 – Living by Faith — 20-23
Day 4 – Praying in Faith — 24-27
Day 5 – The Marriage of Faith and Works — 28-31
Day 6 – Faith in Trials — 32-35
Day 7 – The Power of Faith — 36-39

Day 8 – Let Love be Genuine — 46-49
Day 9 – Be Fervent in Spirit — 50-53
Day 10 – Rejoice in Hope — 54-57
Day 11 – Bless Those Who Persecute You — 58-61
Day 12 – Rejoicing and Weeping with Others — 62-65
Day 13 – Live in Harmony — 66-69
Day 14 – Overcome Evil with Good — 70-73

Day 15 – Encountering God through Faith — 80-83
Day 16 – Encountering God through Prayer — 84-87
Day 17 – Encountering God through Thanksgiving — 88-91
Day 18 – Encountering God through Worship — 92-95
Day 19 – Encountering God through Scripture — 96-99
Day 20 – Encountering God through the Receiving of His Presence — 100-103
Day 21 – Encountering God through Others — 104-107

Day 22 – God's Heart to Meet with David — 114-117
Day 23 – God's Heart to Meet with Gideon — 118-120
Day 24 – God's Heart to Meet with Moses — 122-125
Day 25 – God's Heart to Meet with Man: Jesus to Us — 126-129
Day 26 – God's Heart to Meet with Man: the Woman Caught in Adultery — 130-133
Day 27 – God's Heart to Meet with Man at Pentecost — 134-137
Day 28 – God's Heart to Meet with Man: John on Patmos — 138-141

DAYS 1 - 7

Faith

01

WEEK

"For by grace you have been saved through faith. And this is not your own doing; it is the gift of God." Ephesians 2:8

WEEKLY OVERVIEW

Hebrews 11:1 says, *"Now faith is the assurance of things hoped for, the conviction of things not seen."* Faith is the undercurrent of everything we do as followers of Jesus. Without faith we lose all that Christ died to give us while here on earth. It is by faith we access the peace, joy, guidance, love, and purpose that comes from restored relationship with our heavenly Father. As we seek an increase in faith in response to God's faithfulness this week, may you experience a greater depth of intimacy with your living, Almighty, and loving heavenly Father.

At the Heart of Faith

DAY 1

DEVOTIONAL

As believers living our lives founded on the hope given to us by God, faith is our lifeblood. Without faith we have nothing. Without faith, all sense of purpose, value, and joy in present trials and circumstances scatters as dust in the wind. But with faith we discover a wellspring of life with its origins found in the faithfulness of our Creator God. With faith we experience the effects of promises made to us by our living, loving, active, and trustworthy heavenly Father. With faith the abundant life God desires for us is removed from a shroud of doubt, fear, and hopelessness and becomes our reality. So what's at the heart of this incredible gift of faith? How do we as children of God access the life-giving fruits of faith?

The Bible defines faith as *"the assurance of things hoped for, the conviction of things not seen"* (Hebrews 11:1). Hebrews 11 continues in verses 2-7 saying,

For by it the people of old received their commendation. By faith we understand that the universe was created by the word of God, so that what is seen was not made out of things that are visible. By faith Abel offered to God a more acceptable sacrifice than Cain, through which he was commended as righteous, God commending him by accepting his gifts. And through his faith, though he died, he still speaks. By faith Enoch was taken up so that he should not see death, and he was not found, because God had taken him. Now before he was taken

> *"That your faith might not rest in the wisdom of men but in the power of God."*
>
> **1 CORINTHIANS 2:5**

he was commended as having pleased God. And without faith it is impossible to please him, for whoever would draw near to God must believe that he exists and that he rewards those who seek him. By faith Noah, being warned by God concerning events as yet unseen, in reverent fear constructed an ark for the saving of his household. By this he condemned the world and became an heir of the righteousness that comes by faith.

Hebrews 11 tells us that faith is simply this: trusting in our God who is completely and altogether faithful. Faith is the natural response to a revelation of God's faithfulness.

We are to live entirely by faith, or entirely in response to God's faithfulness. Every action, thought, emotion, word, and perspective is meant to be founded on the faithfulness of our heavenly Father. Abel offered a more acceptable sacrifice because he had a greater revelation and trust of God's faithfulness. Enoch was saved from earthly death because he pleased God with his faith. Hebrews 11:6 makes it abundantly clear: *"Without faith it is impossible to please him, for whoever would draw near to God must believe that he exists and that he rewards those who seek him."* We are to believe in the reality of God and to trust that he will reward us when we seek him. In other words, we are to live our lives entirely out of the revelation of God's faithfulness. And Romans 4:20-21 says in reference to Abraham, *"No unbelief made him waver concerning the promise of God, but he grew strong in his faith as he gave glory to God, fully convinced that God was able to do what he had promised."* We are to be children convinced of the overwhelming ability of God to move and work in our lives.

Where do you lack faith today? What areas of your life have you taken into your own hands? Where are you full of fear, anxiety, depression, or hopelessness today? Know that the path to faith in those areas is paved with fresh revelation of God's faithfulness. 2 Timothy 2:13 says, *"If we are faithless, he remains faithful—for he cannot deny himself."* Your God will always be faithful to you. You can trust him with any problem you are going through. He longs to work in your favor.

Seek out a greater understanding of your God's faithfulness and allow your heart to be transformed. Spend time in prayer meditating on the character of your heavenly Father and allowing the Holy Spirit to do a work in your heart on a level that would fill you with the ability and desire to live entirely in faith.

GUIDED PRAYER

1. Meditate on how Scripture defines faith.

"No unbelief made him waver concerning the promise of God, but he grew strong in his faith as he gave glory to God, fully convinced that God was able to do what he had promised." Romans 4:20-21

"That your faith might not rest in the wisdom of men but in the power of God." 1 Corinthians 2:5

"Now faith is the assurance of things hoped for, the conviction of things not seen." Hebrews 11:1

2. Reflect on any areas in your own life where you struggle with faith. What areas do you seem to live out in your own strength? What anxiety or fear consistently comes against you?

3. Meditate on the faithfulness of your heavenly Father. Allow God's faithfulness to wash away any fear or anxiety you struggle with. Allow his amazing character to fill you with hope, joy, and peace.

"If we are faithless, he remains faithful—for he cannot deny himself." 2 Timothy 2:13

"God is faithful, by whom you were called into the fellowship of his Son, Jesus Christ our Lord." 1 Corinthians 1:9

"For the word of the Lord is upright, and all his work is done in faithfulness." Psalm 33:4

"Your steadfast love, O Lord, extends to the heavens, your faithfulness to the clouds." Psalm 36:5

The Scriptures declaring the faithfulness of God go on and on. All of the earth finds its life as the result of God's faithfulness to his promises. We live and breathe by the goodness and love of our God. God longs to give you a tangible story of his faithfulness. He longs to work in your life specifically and uniquely. Open up your life to him, ask him for his help, and watch as he works faithfully in your midst. Your God loves you, cares about you, and is for you. May you experience the abundant life only faith can bring you today.

Extended Reading: Hebrews 11

Faith Comes by Hearing

DAY 2

DEVOTIONAL

Romans 10:17 says, *"Faith comes from hearing, and hearing through the word of Christ."* Scripture offers us every truth we need to live a lifestyle of faith. Within its pages are powerful stories describing the miraculous works of a God who remained faithful to a people who chose pride, selfishness, and rebellion over his perfect, loving ways. And it contains incredible moments where God's people responded to his faithfulness with faith and were greatly rewarded.

*"So faith comes from hearing, and
hearing through the word of Christ."*

ROMANS 10:17

Proverbs 4:20-22 says, *"My son, be attentive to my words; incline your ear to my sayings. Let them not escape from your sight; keep them within your heart. For they are life to those who find them, and healing to all their flesh."* The desire of God for you and me is to be children filled with his life-giving words. God longs for us to experience the joy, purpose, and peace of faith founded on his word. He longs for us to live our lives with Scripture as a constant source of hope when the world seems to be crashing down around us.

For a long time, the Bible bored me. I knew I should read it so I would try and make some time here and there to read a little bit. But it felt more like an assignment than an encounter with the powerful words of God. It wasn't until I began to read Scripture as an avenue to connect with God and have my life transformed that I began to enjoy it. As I began to allow God's word to fill me with faith to live differently, I discovered the power of the Bible.

When I used Scripture as a way to learn about and connect to the heart of my heavenly Father, my desire to read it grew to the point of overflowing.

Scripture has the power to lead us to a different way of living: the way of faith. Stories like Abraham and Isaac should guide us to trust the promises of our God. Stories like Israel and the walls of Jericho should lead us to act on God's word and leadership in faith that he will move in powerful ways to destroy our seemingly insurmountable obstacles. And the life, death, and resurrection of Jesus should guide us to a life of service to our God who would give up everything just to have restored relationship with us.

May your faith be stirred today in the reading of Scripture. May the pages of God's word guide you to a lifestyle of trust, hope, and surrender. And may you experience the joy of living by faith in response to your God's amazing acts of faithfulness.

GUIDED PRAYER

1. Meditate on the ability of God's word to fill you with faith.

"So faith comes from hearing, and hearing through the word of Christ." Romans 10:17

"My son, be attentive to my words; incline your ear to my sayings. Let them not escape from your sight; keep them within your heart. For they are life to those who find them, and healing to all their flesh." Proverbs 4:20-22

2. Where do you need faith today? What problem or obstacle seems insurmountable before you? Where do you need hope and joy?

3. Meditate on Scripture in reference to your need. Find a story that will fill you with faith for the problem set before you.

"My son, do not forget my teaching, but let your heart keep my commandments, for length of days and years of life and peace they will add to you. Let not steadfast love and faithfulness forsake you; bind them around your neck; write them on the tablet of your heart. So you will find favor and good success in the sight of God and man. Trust in the Lord with all your heart, and do not lean on your own understanding." Proverbs 3:1-5

The story of Jesus walking on water in Matthew 14:28-33 serves as a great example of life lived in faith and in doubt. May we be a people who live in full faith and stand on the unshakable truth of God's word.

And Peter answered him, "Lord, if it is you, command me to come to you on the water." He said, "Come." So Peter got out of the boat and walked on the water and came to Jesus. But when he saw the wind, he was afraid, and beginning to sink he cried out, "Lord, save me." Jesus immediately reached out his hand and took hold of him, saying to him, "O you of little faith, why did you doubt?" And when they got into the boat, the wind ceased. And those in the boat worshiped him, saying, "Truly you are the Son of God."

Extended Reading: Romans 5

WEEK 1

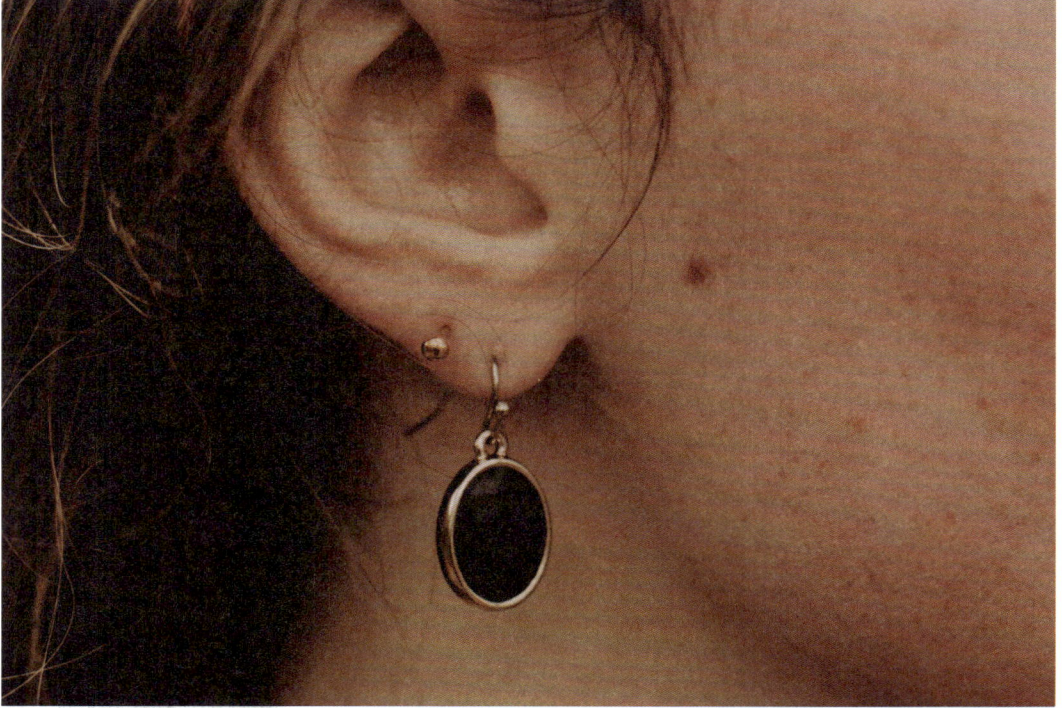

Living by Faith

DAY 3

DEVOTIONAL

Living by faith is the key that unlocks the door to the fullness of God's promises. There is no doubt that God will always be faithful to his promises. Scripture is clear in 2 Timothy 2:13 that *"if we are faithless, he remains faithful—for he cannot deny himself."* Faithfulness is within God's nature. But, without faith we will not experience the fullness of what is available to us in God's promises. God does not force emotion on us. He does not force us to receive the joy and peace that comes through trusting him. He does not force us into the fullness of relationship available to us in faith. And he does not force his purposes on us. Faith is the vehicle by which we experience all that God longs to give us. Specifically, faith is the avenue on which we experience the fullness of God's promises for intimacy with him, purpose in this life, and freedom from sin.

Hebrews 10:19-22 says, *"Therefore, brothers, since we have confidence to enter the holy places by the blood of Jesus, by the new and living way that he opened for us through the curtain, that is, through his flesh, and since we have a great priest over the house of God, let us draw near with a true heart in full assurance of faith, with our hearts sprinkled clean from an evil conscience and our bodies washed with pure water."* By faith we walk into God's presence. In faith we believe God desires to be with us. Experiencing the fullness of restored relationship with our heavenly Father requires a heart full of faith and trust that God longs to tangibly be with us, his children. Without faith we will live solely for the pleasures this world has to offer and miss out on all the satisfaction of living this life for and with God above all else. In faith we can experience all the intimacy available to us through the life, death, and resurrection of Jesus.

Hebrews 11:32-34 says, *"And what more shall I say? For time would fail me to tell of Gideon, Barak, Samson, Jephthah, of David and Samuel and the prophets—who through faith conquered kingdoms, enforced justice,*

"For we walk by faith, not by sight."

2 CORINTHIANS 5:7

obtained promises, stopped the mouths of lions, quenched the power of fire, escaped the edge of the sword, were made strong out of weakness, became mighty in war, put foreign armies to flight."* We've been sent out by Jesus to make disciples of all nations. We've been given a command to bring light into the darkness everywhere we go. You and I have been given a purpose of eternal value and of great importance to our Lord and King. And Hebrews 11 is clear that it is by faith that the works of God are done. When we live by faith we bring the kingdom of God into every dark corner around us. When we live by faith we invite the Holy Spirit to work in and through every situation to draw others to himself. It's in faith that we find our purpose.

And finally, Ephesians 6:16 says, *"In all circumstances take up the shield of faith, with which you can extinguish all the flaming darts of the evil one."* It is through faith that we walk in the freedom from sin available to us by the promise of God. As children of God wrapped up in the finished work of Christ, we have been set free from the bondage of sin. By the power of Jesus' death on the cross, you and I never have to sin again. But Paul teaches us in Ephesians that it is through faith that we extinguish the flaming darts of the evil one. If we don't trust God at his word that we who were completely entangled to the schemes of the enemy by sin are now considered the righteousness of God (2 Corinthians 5:21), we will not walk in freedom. It is through faith that we renew our mind and experience the wonderful freedom from sin available to us.

We all need a greater measure of intimacy with God, purpose, and freedom from sin. Not one of us has experienced all that is available to us through faith. May you seek out all that God has in store for you if you will take him at his word and trust him in response to his faithfulness. Spend time in prayer receiving all that God longs to give you by faith.

GUIDED PRAYER

1. Meditate on all that is available to you in the lifestyle of faith.

"And without faith it is impossible to please him, for whoever would draw near to God must believe that he exists and that he rewards those who seek him." Hebrews 11:6

"And what more shall I say? For time would fail me to tell of Gideon, Barak, Samson, Jephthah, of David and Samuel and the prophets—who through faith conquered kingdoms, enforced justice, obtained promises, stopped the mouths of lions, quenched the power of fire, escaped the edge of the sword, were made strong out of weakness, became mighty in war, put foreign armies to flight." Hebrews 11:32-34

"In all circumstances take up the shield of faith, with which you can extinguish all the flaming darts of the evil one." Ephesians 6:16

2. Ask God to lead you to a greater measure of faith. Ask him to give you the faith to pursue intimacy with him, his purposes, and freedom from sin. Listen to all that he would say to you in these quiet moments. Let him give you a fresh perspective of what it is to live by faith.

3. Pursue all that is available to you today in the promises of God. What new levels of relationship does God long to lead you to? What new purposes does he have in store for you? What freedom does he long to bring you?

May you be filled with hunger for the deeper things of God today. And may you have the courage and tenacity to seek out everything God has in store for you. If you will pursue him with all your heart in faith you will discover all that your heart has been searching for. He has adventure, excitement, joy, fulfillment, and love for all who live by faith. Today is the day to live in the newness of life Jesus died for you to have.

Extended Reading: 2 Corinthians 5

Praying in Faith

DAY 4

DEVOTIONAL

Prayer is our most powerful gift when done in faith. E. M. Bounds described the power of prayer in saying, "We can do nothing without prayer. All things can be done by importunate prayer. It surmounts or removes all obstacles, overcomes every resisting force and gains its ends in the face of invincible hindrances." God loves to move when we pray. He is not a God who forces his will on his people, but in

> *"Have faith in God. Truly, I say to you, whoever says to this mountain, 'Be taken up and thrown into the sea,' and does not doubt in his heart, but believes that what he says will come to pass, it will be done for him. Therefore I tell you, whatever you ask in prayer, believe that you have received it, and it will be yours."*
>
> **MARK 11:22-24**

love waits for us to capture his heart and ask him to move and work in our lives and the lives of others. There is no more important task before us today than to learn what it is to pray in faith.

Mark 11:22-24 says, *"Have faith in God. Truly, I say to you, whoever says to this mountain, 'Be taken up and thrown into the sea,' and does not doubt in his heart, but believes that what he says will come to pass, it will be done for him. Therefore I tell you, whatever you ask in prayer, believe that you have received it, and it will be yours."* Jesus illustrates an important link between prayer and faith. When we have faith that God will move as he has told us he would and we pray in response to that faith, the impossible happens.

Conversely James 1:5-8 says, *"If any of you lacks wisdom, let him ask God, who gives generously to all without reproach, and it will be given him. But let him ask in faith, with no doubting, for the one who doubts is like a wave of the sea that is driven and tossed by the wind. For that person must not suppose that he will receive anything from the Lord; he is a double-minded man, unstable in all his ways."* Where faith positions us to receive from God, doubt has the opposite effect. Scripture is clear that the prayers God responds to are prayers of faith. God has given us purpose here. He longs to co-labor with his people. Our job is to capture his heart by spending time in his presence and pray boldly in response to his faithfulness.

You and I have been given the incredible gift of conversation with a God who longs to move in response to our prayers. What obstacles stand in your way today? Where do you need a miracle? Who needs prayer around you? Spend time capturing the heart of your heavenly Father and praying with boldness. He waits to respond to your prayers and do the work only he can do.

GUIDED PRAYER

1. Meditate on the power of prayer in faith.

"Have faith in God. Truly, I say to you, whoever says to this mountain, 'Be taken up and thrown into the sea,' and does not doubt in his heart, but believes that what he says will come to pass, it will be done for him. Therefore I tell you, whatever you ask in prayer, believe that you have received it, and it will be yours." Mark 11:22-24

"Truly, I say to you, if you have faith and do not doubt, you will not only do what has been done to the fig tree, but even if you say to this mountain, 'Be taken up and thrown into the sea,' it will happen. And whatever you ask in prayer, you will receive, if you have faith." Matthew 21:21-22

2. Reflect on your life. What obstacles stand in your way? Where do you need God to work? Who around you needs the power of your prayer today?

3. Ask God what he thinks about the situations in which you desire to pray and then pray boldly according to his will. Seek out Scripture and pray in line with God's word. Have faith that God will move according to his word in response to your prayer of faith.

Often we are turned off to the idea of praying boldly when we feel God hasn't answered our prayers in the past. Don't let past experience stand in the way of living your life in total alignment with the word of God. We will never fully understand all of God's ways. All we can do is live as he has led us and trust in him. Scripture is clear that God cares for you and longs to help you. He desires to move and work in your midst on a daily basis. Have faith in your heavenly Father and pray to him boldly today.

Extended Reading: Mark 11

The Marriage of Faith and Works

DAY 5

DEVOTIONAL

"Work" typically has a negative connotation in my mind. I associate work with something I have to do but don't feel like doing. I separate out work from play or fun. But with God, the word "work" couldn't be more different. Work is designed to be the expression of our abundant, life-giving relationship with our heavenly Father. God

> *"For as the body apart from the spirit is dead,*
> *so also faith apart from works is dead."*
>
> **JAMES 2:26**

doesn't call us to work out of obligation or to earn his love, but to live our lives in response to his love. It's for this reason that Scripture is clear about God's intention for the marriage of faith and works.

James 2:26 says, *"For as the body apart from the spirit is dead, so also faith apart from works is dead."* What is our faith if it doesn't produce action? What is the nature of our relationship with God if it doesn't cause us to live differently? Often we have a misunderstanding about what it is God would have us do if we were to truly submit our life fully to him. And our misunderstanding veils our heart from receiving the fullness of life and enjoyment of the work God intends for us.

Often we believe if we were really to hand over our life to God in faith he would call us to do a lot of things we don't want to do. Maybe we believe he'd call us to a foreign mission field, to make little to no money, or simply to live our lives awkwardly and intrusively. If you only remember one thing today, remember this: God will only ever lead you to a life perfectly, uniquely, and wonderfully designed to bring you and others around you the utmost fulfillment, purpose, passion, and joy. Everything he calls you to he intends to use to satisfy the desires of your heart. Maybe he is calling you to something you don't fully understand yet, but if you will say yes to him, the very calling that you possibly feared most will be the satisfaction of a dream you didn't know you had.

God calls us to a life of works because he loves us and has designed us for such a purpose. Ephesians 2:10 says, *"For we are his workmanship, created in Christ Jesus for good works, which God prepared beforehand, that we should walk in them."* The work he is calling you to is perfect for you because he is the one who formed you and knows you. Have faith in the love and perfect will of your heavenly Father. Choose to live a life of good works. And experience the joy of living every minute of your day with intentional and eternal purpose.

Spend time in prayer allowing the word and character of God to renew your mind on the subject of faith and works. Allow the Holy Spirit to fill you with a desire to live a life of good works today in light of God's love for you.

30

GUIDED PRAYER

1. Meditate on the marriage of faith and works. Renew your mind to the goodness of work.

"For as the body apart from the spirit is dead, so also faith apart from works is dead." James 2:26

"And let our people learn to devote themselves to good works, so as to help cases of urgent need, and not be unfruitful." Titus 3:14

"For we are his workmanship, created in Christ Jesus for good works, which God prepared beforehand, that we should walk in them." Ephesians 2:10

2. Ask the Holy Spirit to reveal to you what works he has laid before you today. Hand over to him the tasks set before you and ask him to fill you with the knowledge of how he would have you accomplish them.

3. Commit to living today with a renewed perspective on work. Work is joyful and life-giving when we do it with the Holy Spirit. Choose to live your life in line with God's intention for you and enjoy the work set before you!

"In the same way, let your light shine before others, so that they may see your good works and give glory to your Father who is in heaven." Matthew 5:16

What would your life look like if you chose to do your work filled with the joy and purpose of the Holy Spirit? The fruit of the Spirit is just as available to you during work as it is at any other time of the day! All you have to do is choose to live your life with a different perspective than others around you. Take hardships to God and ask him for his heart! Enjoy your days working and bearing the fruit of your faith.

Extended Reading: James 2

Faith in Trials

DAY 6

DEVOTIONAL

Trials and tribulations have the power to either keep us from abundant life or produce in us character that sustains abundant life. The choice is up to us. Will our faith remain steadfast in the face of trouble or will we abandon the lifestyle of faith for one of the world?

> *"Count it all joy, my brothers, when you meet trials of various kinds, for you know that the testing of your faith produces steadfastness. And let steadfastness have its full effect, that you may be perfect and complete, lacking in nothing."*
>
> **JAMES 1:2-4**

James 1:2-4 says, *"Count it all joy, my brothers, when you meet trials of various kinds, for you know that the testing of your faith produces steadfastness. And let steadfastness have its full effect, that you may be perfect and complete, lacking in nothing."* Allow the phrase, *"Count it all joy"* to settle in for a second. What trials have you faced in the past? What trials stand before you today? Is joy the emotion that stirs up within you when you think about your problems?

My first instinct in the face of trial is to run. I long to abandon the problems before me, to act as if they don't exist. But Scripture commands me to count my trials as joy and run at them head-on for the sake of being transformed into a faith-filled, steadfast child of God. God sees trials as a chance to produce character within me, not as a circumstance intended to harm me or derail his plans for my life.

The greatest gift we've been given in the face of trials is faith. When problems are staring at us head-on it's hard to see around them to the beneficial outcome God intends. In order to face trials the way God intends, we must have faith. We have to believe that God has an outcome as beneficial as the trial is hard. We have to have faith that God will see us through every problem that stands in our way and produce in us a steadfastness on which we can experience abundant life.

Hebrews 10:35-39 says, *"Therefore do not throw away your confidence, which has a great reward. For you have need of endurance, so that when you have done the will of God you may receive what is promised. For, 'Yet a little while, and the coming one will come and will not delay; but my righteous one shall live by faith, and if he shrinks back, my soul has no pleasure in him.' But we are not of those who shrink back and are destroyed, but of those who have faith and preserve their souls."* May we not be a people who shrink back but stand on the firm ground of God's promises. May we be believers filled with faith founded on the faithfulness of God.

Spend time in prayer allowing God's word to fill you with fresh perspective about your trials and tribulations.

GUIDED PRAYER

1. Meditate on God's desire to use trials for your benefit.

"Count it all joy, my brothers, when you meet trials of various kinds, for you know that the testing of your faith produces steadfastness. And let steadfastness have its full effect, that you may be perfect and complete, lacking in nothing." James 1:2-4

"And we desire each one of you to show the same earnestness to have the full assurance of hope until the end, so that you may not be sluggish, but imitators of those who through faith and patience inherit the promises." Hebrews 6:11-12

"For I consider that the sufferings of this present time are not worth comparing with the glory that is to be revealed to us." Romans 8:18

2. Reflect on the trials standing before you.
What insurmountable problem is weighing on you? What job, relationship, or circumstance troubles you?

3. Ask God to fill you with faith in response to the trial before you. Allow the Holy Spirit to reveal to you his plans to use the trial for your good. Ask him to show you what characteristic he longs to produce in you. And ask him to fill you with the strength and courage to face your trial head-on and overcome it.

May 1 Peter 1:6-9 be the passage you stand on when trials rise up around you today:

In this you rejoice, though now for a little while, if necessary, you have been grieved by various trials, so that the tested genuineness of your faith—more precious than gold that perishes though it is tested by fire—may be found to result in praise and glory and honor at the revelation of Jesus Christ. Though you have not seen him, you love him. Though you do not now see him, you believe in him and rejoice with joy that is inexpressible and filled with glory, obtaining the outcome of your faith, the salvation of your souls.

Extended Reading: James 1

The Power of Faith

DAY 7

DEVOTIONAL

The Holy Spirit loves to move with power in response to faith. Hebrews 11:30 tells us, *"By faith the walls of Jericho fell down after they had been encircled for seven days."* Hebrews 11:32-33 says, *"For time would fail me to tell of Gideon, Barak, Samson, Jephthah, of David and Samuel and*

> *"By faith the walls of Jericho fell down after they had been encircled for seven days."*
>
> **HEBREWS 11:30**

the prophets—Who through faith conquered kingdoms, enforced justice, obtained promises, stopped the mouths of lions." As we conclude this week on living by faith, I believe God would fill us with a fresh revelation of his power. Let's open our hearts and minds to receive all that God would reveal to us about his power and invite him to work in our midst in faith today.

We serve the Creator of all. 1 Chronicles 29:11 says, *"Yours, O Lord, is the greatness and the power and the glory and the victory and the majesty, for all that is in the heavens and in the earth is yours. Yours is the kingdom, O Lord, and you are exalted as head above all."* And throughout Scripture we see God using his power in response to the faith of his people. Whether it be the walls of Jericho tumbling down into rubble or the lame man at the temple gate called Beautiful jumping to his feet, God clearly moves in powerful ways when his people live by faith.

Jesus even promises in Matthew 17:20, *"If you have faith like a grain of mustard seed, you will say to this mountain, 'Move from here to there,' and it will move, and nothing will be impossible for you."* If we have the smallest amount of faith, Jesus says, *"Nothing will be impossible"* for us. The God who formed every mountain, valley, river, ocean, and person has told you that he will fight on your behalf in response to your faith.

David was an incredible example of a child of God filled with the faith and powerful work of God. David was constantly in need of God's help. From stepping up to slay Goliath in faith to escaping pursuers, he exemplified what it was to live constantly in the power of faith. David wrote in Psalm 3:1-6, *"O Lord, how many are my foes! Many are rising against me; many are saying of my soul, there is no salvation for him in God. But you, O Lord, are a shield about me, my glory, and the lifter of my head. I cried aloud to the Lord, and he answered me from his holy hill. I lay down and slept; I woke again, for the Lord sustained me. I will not be afraid of many thousands of people who have set themselves against me all around."* David knew of the power of God when he asked for God's help. So great was his faith in God's ability and desire to come to his aid that he found rest and security in the face of thousands of enemies.

You are the child of the Most High, all-powerful God. May your life be marked by the power of your faithful heavenly Father.

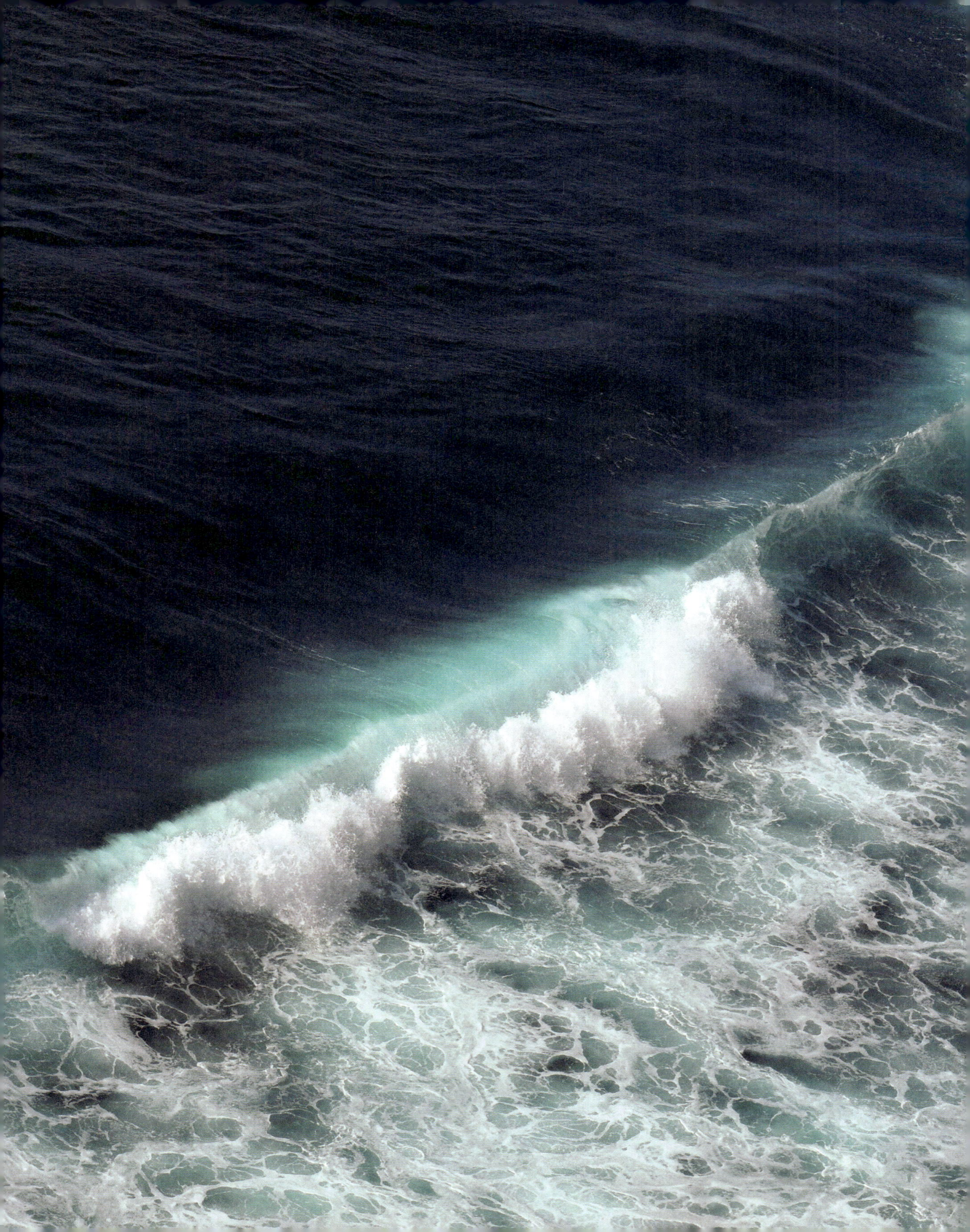

GUIDED PRAYER

1. Meditate on the power of faith.

"By faith the walls of Jericho fell down after they had been encircled for seven days." Hebrews 11:30

"For time would fail me to tell of Gideon, Barak, Samson, Jephthah, of David and Samuel and the prophets—Who through faith conquered kingdoms, enforced justice, obtained promises, stopped the mouths of lions." Hebrews 11:32-33

"For truly, I say to you, if you have faith like a grain of mustard seed, you will say to this mountain, 'Move from here to there,' and it will move, and nothing will be impossible for you." Matthew 17:20

2. Where do you need the power of God in your life?
Where do you need the help of your heavenly Father?

3. In faith ask God to move in mighty, specific ways.
Come before your heavenly Father boldly and ask him to make his reality, power, and love known in your life.

There is no pride in living your life in line with God's word. It isn't haughty or selfish for you to have faith for God to work in your midst. God loves you and longs to help you. He has perfect plans to work in and through every circumstance in your life. Have faith in the love, mercy, and power of your God today.

Extended Reading: Psalm 3

DAYS 8 - 14

The marks of a true Christian

02

WEEK

"But the fruit of the Spirit is love, joy, peace, patience, kindness, goodness, faithfulness, gentleness, self-control; against such things there is no law." Galatians 5:22-23

WEEKLY OVERVIEW

This week we're going to take a look at seven principles found in Romans 12 that describe the marks of a true Christian. The intent of studying this passage is not to condemn or lead you to comparison. Instead, let Paul's teaching fill you with a deep, transformative longing to wholeheartedly pursue the life of faith God intends for you. Ask God to help you see yourself as he sees you, to see the grace he's placed upon your life by the blood of Jesus so that you might walk more fully in the power and anointing of the Spirit. Open your heart to God, and let him do a mighty work in you. He is near to you, ready to mold and shape you into a disciple filled with and fueled by his incredible love. May you discover God's grace and perspective this week as you examine your life in light of this powerful passage of Scripture.

Let Love be Genuine

DAY 8

DEVOTIONAL

Paul begins his description of what it looks like to be a true disciple of Christ in Romans 12 with a foundational phrase for this passage: *"Let love be genuine."* Genuine love is one of the most powerful forces in all of creation. Genuine love drove Jesus through his life, death, and resurrection. Genuine love started the advance of the gospel, leading to the salvation of billions. The world tirelessly searches for genuine love. And it is genuine love that is meant to set you and me apart as disciples of Jesus. Scripture says in 1 John 4:7-11:

Beloved, let us love one another, for love is from God, and whoever loves has been born of God and knows God. Anyone who does not love does not know God, because God is love. In this the love of God was made manifest among us, that God sent his only Son into the world, so that we might live through him. In this is love, not that we have loved God but that he loved us and sent his Son to be the propitiation for our sins. Beloved, if God so loved us, we also ought to love one another.

Paul sums up his beautiful description of love in 1 Corinthians 13:13 this way: *"So now faith, hope, and love abide, these three; but the greatest of these is love."* And Jesus, when asked what the greatest commandment is, said, *"You shall love the Lord your God with all your heart and with all your soul and with all your mind. This is the great and first commandment.*

"Let love be genuine. Abhor what is evil; hold fast to what is good. Love one another with brotherly affection. Outdo one another in showing honor."

ROMANS 12:9-10

And a second is like it: You shall love your neighbor as yourself. On these two commandments depend all the Law and the Prophets" (Matthew 22:37-40).

You were created to give and receive love. Love is your highest calling. God has set you apart to minister to others, sharing the genuine love you've been shown. It's only in living for love that you will truly find peace and purpose. It's only in the giving and receiving of genuine love that you will feel whole and satisfied. The Bible is clear about God's plan for you. God intends to pour his love out over you to the level of overflowing, enabling others to get a glimpse of his vast love for them through your life.

So, how can you be a person who shows genuine love to those around you? What does a life lived for love look like? It starts with spending time daily encountering the vast ocean of God's love for you. In John 13:34, Jesus says, *"A new commandment I give to you, that you love one another: just as I have loved you, you also are to love one another."* The disciples could only love each other because they had experienced firsthand the incredible love of Jesus. You will not be able to love genuinely if you aren't receiving God's love for yourself. You must take time every day to simply encounter the love of your heavenly Father. His love is designed to lay the foundation for the good works you do. He never intends for you to give what you haven't received. Romans 12:9-10 proves to be great instruction for living a life of genuine love. Paul writes, *"Let love be genuine. Abhor what is evil; hold fast to what is good. Love one another with brotherly affection. Outdo one another in showing honor."* Choose to engage in good over evil. Fill your life with all that is good. Show grace and respect to others because that is what your heavenly Father has done for you. Live a life of outdoing those around you in showing love and honor.

God has chosen to reveal his love to the world through your life. He's committed to using you to bring others to himself. And he has a perfect plan to mold and shape you through his love into a person who naturally shows genuine love to others out of the overflow of God's love in your own life. You don't need to place the weight of others' salvation on your shoulders. Instead, encounter the love God has for you today. Let his perspective of you change the way you see yourself and others. And simply love those around you with the love you've been shown. Choose to live a life of genuine love today and find out just how broad, long, high, and deep is the love of Christ for both you and others around you (Ephesians 3:18-19).

GUIDED PRAYER

1. Spend time receiving God's love for you. Ask him to make his nearness known to you. Let his presence fill up the places of your heart that need a fresh encounter with him.

"That according to the riches of his glory he may grant you to be strengthened with power through his Spirit in your inner being, so that Christ may dwell in your hearts through faith—that you, being rooted and grounded in love, may have strength to comprehend with all the saints what is the breadth and length and height and depth, and to know the love of Christ that surpasses knowledge, that you may be filled with all the fullness of God." Ephesians 3:16-19

2. Ask God to give you a fresh revelation of how he sees you. Ask him to mold and shape you into the person he would have you be. Allow his grace and love to transform your heart.

3. Now ask the Spirit to help you show genuine love to others. Who around you needs to be genuinely loved by you today? Who needs to be shown honor and respect? Let the love that you've received fill you with the desire and power to love others well.

"A new commandment I give to you, that you love one another: just as I have loved you, you also are to love one another." John 13:34

Extended Reading: 1 John 4

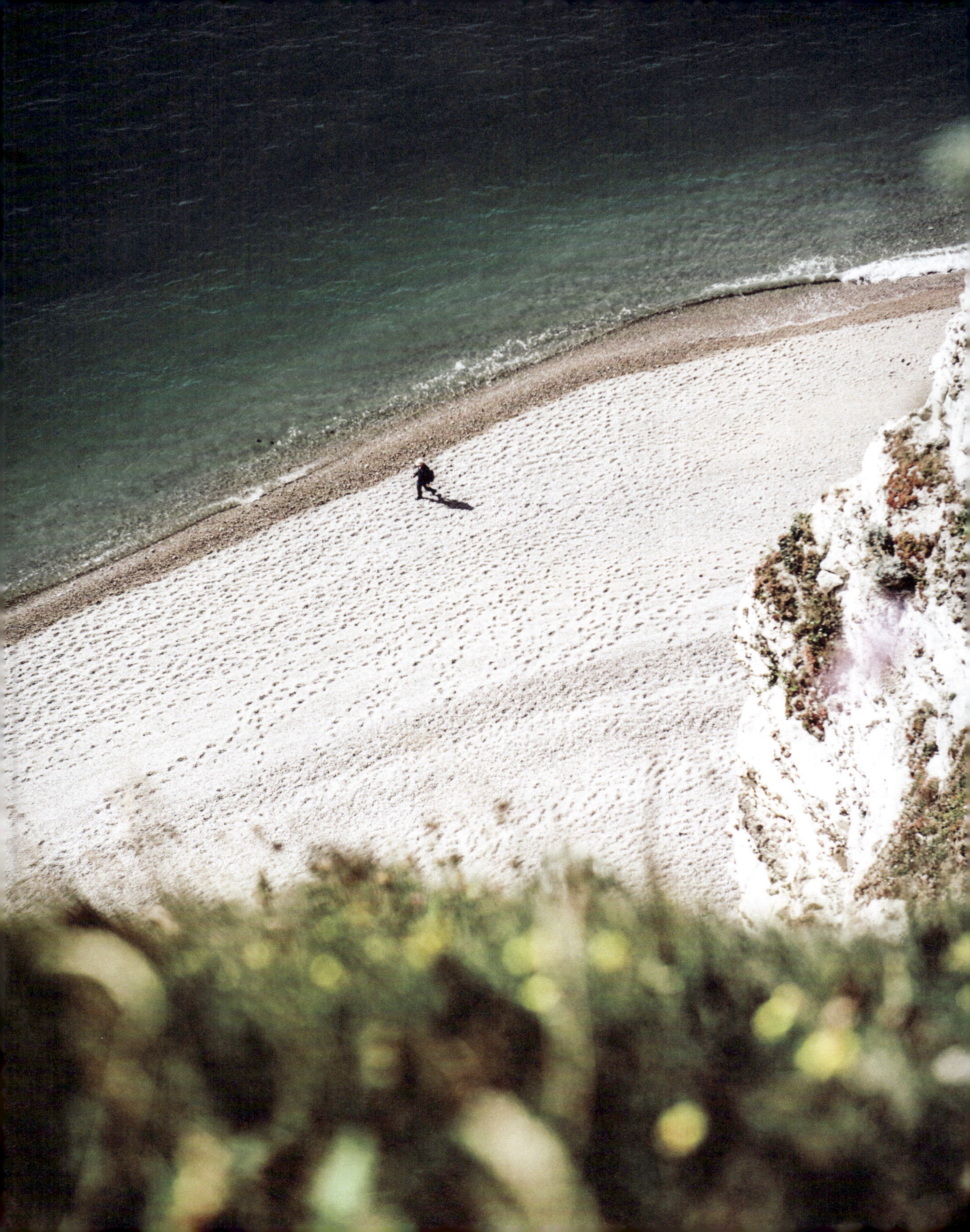

DEVOTIONAL

God shares with us, his disciples, an important command in Romans 12:11. Scripture says, *"Do not be slothful in zeal, be fervent in spirit, serve the Lord."* Do you ever feel slothful in zeal? Here, Paul is talking about feeling sluggish in your relationship with God. He's describing a feeling of laziness, a lack of desire. Do you ever feel like your spirit is anything but fervent? The word fervent here is better translated as *"boiling over."* Do you ever feel like your spirit is more like stagnant water? Let's look today at how

"Do not be slothful in zeal, be fervent in spirit, serve the Lord."

ROMANS 12:11

we as followers of God can stir up our affections for the Lord. Let's make space for God to put fire under any area of our spiritual life that feels stagnant that it might boil over in him.

Foundational to understanding Romans 12:11 is the knowledge that God will never ask you to do something or be something without his help. You are never alone in your spiritual growth. Your job is simply to create space in your heart for God to mold and shape you. Your job is to engage with him and let the Spirit teach, lead, and fill you. Your heavenly Father is near to you. He has a perfect plan to guide you into spiritual growth and fervor. So, in light of that understanding, how can you engage with God and allow him to mold and shape you into a person of greater fervor and zeal?

Psalm 19:7 says, *"The law of the Lord is perfect, reviving the soul."* And Psalm 19:8 says, "The precepts of the Lord are right, rejoicing the heart." Scripture makes clear that to be zealous and fervent in your service to God, you must spend time allowing his word to inflame your spiritual fire. Spending time reading about the depths of God's love for his people, the length he will go for you as his child, and the example of lives empowered by the Spirit will assuredly fill you with passion and zeal. When you spend time in God's word, you are not only reading incredible stories, but hearing the voice of your living and active heavenly Father. Spend time with his word, allowing the voice of God to direct your soul to finding its rest and passion in him.

When you spend time with God, you will naturally be filled with a desire and passion to serve him. Reflect for a moment on how different you feel when you are inflamed with passion in comparison to feeling slothful. You have the power to choose how you will live life every day. You have the choice to engage with God, read his word, spend time in his presence, and allow him to mold and shape you. You also have the power to live a passionless life. The choice is yours. But know God is faithful to fill you with his Spirit every day if you will make space for him to do so. He has total grace for the times you feel sluggish; at the same time he has a perfect plan to lead you out of that state into being *"fervent in spirit."* Engage with God today in prayer. Meditate on his word. Let him fill you with the power and anointing of his Holy Spirit.

The Message translates Romans 12:11 as saying, *"Don't burn out; keep yourselves fueled and aflame. Be alert servants of the Master, cheerfully expectant."* May you experience today the life of a *"cheerfully expectant"* person *"fueled"* and set *"aflame"* by the love and leading of God.

FAITH

GUIDED PRAYER

1. Spend time meditating on God's word. Choose a passage that will stir up your affections for God. Passages like "The High Priestly Prayer" in John 17 are great for encountering God's heart.

2. Now, ask the Holy Spirit to fill you afresh. Spend time in God's presence allowing him to fill you with a desire to serve him.

"Satisfy us in the morning with your steadfast love, that we may rejoice and be glad all our days." Psalm 90:14

3. Ask the Spirit to show you ways you can serve God today. God has a specific plan to use you today to bring spiritual awakening to those around you. He could have you give someone a gift, encourage someone, pray for someone, or even simply engage in conversation with a stranger. Follow the voice of the Spirit as he guides and directs you today.

Finish up the time you spend alone with God today by simply asking his presence to linger with you. Ask him to continually fill you with the flame of his love. Know that wherever you go today he will be there. Whenever you feel sluggish in spirit, he is there to fill you up. Continually engage with him and live today with his grace and love as your foundation and fuel.

Extended Reading: Psalm 43

Rejoice in Hope

DAY 10

DEVOTIONAL

We are not promised a life without struggle here on earth. In fact, the Bible makes clear that the world will hate us for our love of Jesus. John 15:18-19 says, *"If the world hates you, know that it has hated me before it hated you. If you were of the world, the world would love you as its own; but because you are not of the world, but I chose you out of the world, therefore the world hates you."* Jesus even promises us in John 16:33, *"In the world you will have tribulation."* Except John, each disciple was martyred for his faith in Christ, and John was exiled to the prison island of Patmos for preaching that Jesus is God. We live in an imperfect world wrought with the destruction sin and separation from God has caused. You and I will face trials here as followers of Jesus.

In light of Jesus' promise of problems here on earth, it's interesting that Paul would write in Romans 12:12, *"Rejoice in hope, be patient in tribulation, be constant in prayer."* Paul knew all too well the trials we as believers can face in the world, but he wasn't about to let them affect his ability to *"rejoice in hope."* Along with promising us tribulation, Scripture speaks of the perspective we as believers are to have in light of our restored relationship with God. Hebrews 13:14 says, *"For here we have no lasting city, but we seek the city that is to come."* Scripture is clear that this world is not your home. Jesus commands us in Matthew 6:19-21, *"Do not lay up for yourselves treasures on earth, where moth and rust destroy and where thieves break in and steal, but lay up for yourselves treasures in heaven, where neither moth nor rust destroys and where thieves do not break in and steal. For where your treasure is, there your heart will be also."* The Bible doesn't tell us that trials won't hurt here. Being disliked by others or the loss of a loved one, a job, or finances will not feel good. But you can *"rejoice in hope"* and *"be patient in tribulation"* with the knowledge that the trials you suffer here will one day end. Earthly success and possessions are not the goal because *"the world is passing away along with its desires, but whoever does the will of God abides*

> *"Rejoice in hope, be patient in tribulation, be constant in prayer."*
>
> **ROMANS 12:12**

forever" (1 John 2:17). And you are promised an eternity with your heavenly Father where *"death shall be no more, neither shall there be mourning, nor crying, nor pain anymore, for the former things have passed away"* (Revelation 21:4).

So in light of the hope we have in God, how can we be obedient to his word in Romans 12:12? How can we consistently *"rejoice in hope"* and *"be patient in tribulation"* when everything seems to be crashing down around us? Only by being obedient to the last exhortation in Romans 12:12: *"Be constant in prayer."* James 5:13-15 says, *"Is anyone among you suffering? Let him pray. Is anyone cheerful? Let him sing praise. Is anyone among you sick? Let him call for the elders of the church, and let them pray over him, anointing him with oil in the name of the Lord. And the prayer of faith will save the one who is sick, and the Lord will raise him up."* There is power in praying to God. Just as God has answered his children in the past, he will answer you. If you need his peace, pray and ask him for it. If you need to be reminded of what matters, pray and ask for revelation from the Holy Spirit. Humble yourself before your brothers and sisters in Christ and ask for their prayer. *"Be constant in prayer,"* always conversing with your heavenly Father.

God knows what it is to suffer. He knows what it is to go through trial and tribulation. Through every problem, Jesus exemplified what it is to *"rejoice in hope, be patient in tribulation,"* and *"be constant in prayer."* Spend time with Jesus today in prayer. Allow the Spirit to mold and shape you into his likeness. May his love lay an unshakable foundation for you to remain hopeful and patient in every trial and tribulation that comes your way. Jesus says, *"In the world you will have tribulation. But take heart; I have overcome the world"* (John 16:33). In this is our hope: Jesus overcame the world, and so will we. Spend time with the One who has overcome every trial you are going through. Receive his guidance and direction today as you pray.

GUIDED PRAYER

1. Meditate on God's promise of tribulation and the hope you have in Christ Jesus.

"In the world you will have tribulation. But take heart; I have overcome the world." John 16:33

"And the world is passing away along with its desires, but whoever does the will of God abides forever." 1 John 2:17

2. Reflect on any trials or tribulations you are going through. Where do you need hope, patience, and constancy in the midst of trial?

"Rejoice in hope, be patient in tribulation, be constant in prayer." Romans 12:12

3. Now ask the Holy Spirit to strengthen you in the midst of your trials. Place your hope in your God who walks with you through this life. He is near to you.

"Finally, be strong in the Lord and in the strength of his might. Put on the whole armor of God, that you may be able to stand against the schemes of the devil. For we do not wrestle against flesh and blood, but against the rulers, against the authorities, against the cosmic powers over this present darkness, against the spiritual forces of evil in the heavenly places. Therefore take up the whole armor of God, that you may be able to withstand in the evil day, and having done all, to stand firm." Ephesians 6:10-13

You have a real enemy fighting to steal, kill, and destroy you. But *"he who is in you is greater than he who is in the world"* (1 John 4:4). You can overcome by the blood of Jesus. In the Spirit you have a constant source of hope, joy, and power. When you feel the enemy fighting against you, clothe yourself in the armor of God. Stand against him in the authority of Jesus. Rise up, take hold of the temptations and condemnation your enemy brings against you, and throw them at the foot of the cross where Jesus crushed the power of the enemy in your life once and for all.

Extended Reading: John 16

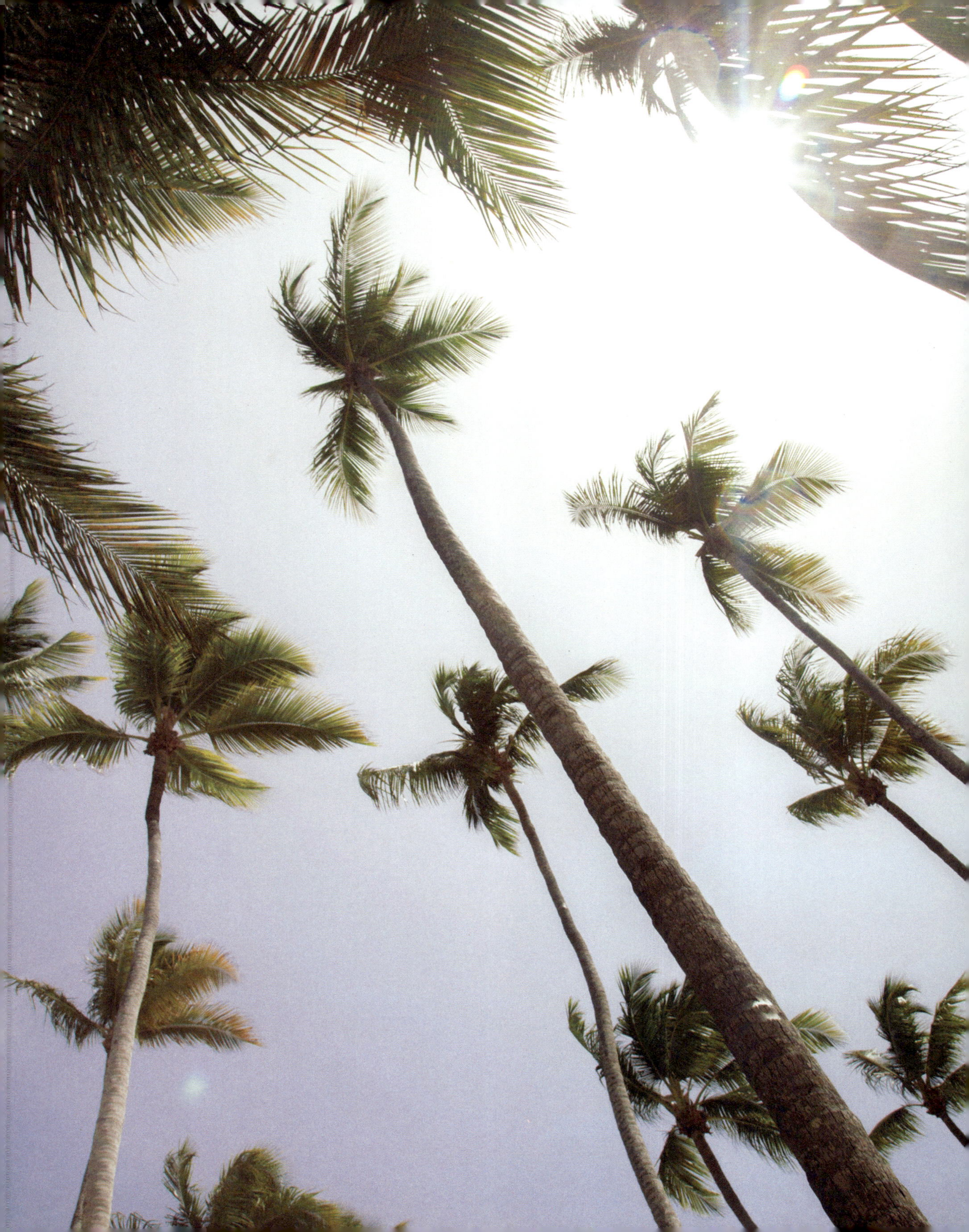

Bless Those Who Persecute You

DAY 11

DEVOTIONAL

Think back on an unresolved conflict you've had. Maybe a friend, spouse, family member, or coworker wronged you. Reflect on the anger, frustration, and sense of injustice you felt. Maybe you still feel those feelings today when you remember that situation. Conflict without grace and forgiveness is like a small hole in the fabric of our emotions that seems to tear larger and larger with every passing day. The more we play the scenario over in our heads, the worse it seems to get. The feelings of unforgiveness and the need for fairness carry with them an increasingly heavy burden. And the Bible teaches us that unforgiveness and seeking fairness are weights we were never intended to bear.

*"Bless those who persecute you;
bless and do not curse them."*

ROMANS 12:14

Jesus completely turned our system of fairness on its head. In Luke 6:27-31, he said, *"But I say to you who hear, Love your enemies, do good to those who hate you, bless those who curse you, pray for those who abuse you. To one who strikes you on the cheek, offer the other also, and from one who takes away your cloak do not withhold your tunic either. Give to everyone who begs from you, and from one who takes away your goods do not demand them back. And as you wish that others would do to you, do so to them."* The way of God is grace-filled, unconditional love, not fighting for what you feel owed. Jesus himself *"did not count equality with God a thing to be grasped, but emptied himself, by taking the form of a servant, being born in the likeness of men. And being found in human form, he humbled himself by becoming obedient to the point of death, even death on a cross"* (Philippians 2:5-8). Jesus chose to never reciprocate the persecution and cursing he faced. Instead, he lived his life in the pursuit of blessing everyone with grace and mercy so that they might know the depth of God's love. And he calls you and me to do the same.

Matthew 5:43-45 says, *"You have heard that it was said, 'You shall love your neighbor and hate your enemy.' But I say to you, Love your enemies and pray for those who persecute you, so that you may be sons of your Father who is in heaven. For he makes his sun rise on the evil and on the good, and sends rain on the just and on the unjust."* We are called to live our lives out of the understanding that we are sons and daughters of God. And Jesus says that loving our enemies and praying for those who persecute us demonstrates our position as God's children. You have been delivered from the world's system of fairness. You no longer have to fight to get what is owed to you. Instead, you can choose to cast off that weight and bless and serve those around you.

"Bless those who persecute you; bless and do not curse them" (Romans 12:14). God will fight for your justice. He will be your protector and defender. Leave those heavy needs at the foot of the cross, and come follow the way of your Savior. The only path to experiencing the fullness of abundant life is choosing to bless your enemies instead of fighting with them. God's path to peace and joy is founded on the concept of grace. When you choose to bless others, even if they don't deserve it, you are choosing to live your life in light of eternity. You have been forgiven and offered grace not because you deserved it, but by the mercy and love of your heavenly Father. Follow the example and teaching of Jesus today, live your life in obedience to his word, and experience the fruit of choosing to bless everyone around you regardless of how they treat you.

FAITH

GUIDED PRAYER

1. Meditate on Jesus' teaching on forgiveness and grace.

"But I say to you who hear, Love your enemies, do good to those who hate you, bless those who curse you, pray for those who abuse you. To one who strikes you on the cheek, offer the other also, and from one who takes away your cloak do not withhold your tunic either. Give to everyone who begs from you, and from one who takes away your goods do not demand them back. And as you wish that others would do to you, do so to them." Luke 6:27-31

2. Now ask the Spirit to fill you with the desire to be like Jesus and obey his word. Trust that God's commands are meant to lead you to the absolute best life you could live.

"Have this mind among yourselves, which is yours in Christ Jesus, who, though he was in the form of God, did not count equality with God a thing to be grasped, but emptied himself, by taking the form of a servant, being born in the likeness of men. And being found in human form, he humbled himself by becoming obedient to the point of death, even death on a cross." Philippians 2:5-8

3. Spend time in God's presence, allowing the love and grace he offers you to mold and shape you into the likeness of Jesus. The more time you spend with God, the more you will become like him. Rest in his nearness.

Blessing those who have hurt you is one of the hardest things to do as a believer. It requires the perspective and fortitude to choose God's ways over what feels most gratifying at the time. But you have the power to choose the abundant life God makes available to you in every moment. The Holy Spirit will help you forgive and offer grace to others if you will allow him to. Choose to bless those who persecute you today, and watch as the love and honor you show others brings heaven to earth around you.

Extended Reading: Matthew 5

Rejoicing and Weeping with Others

DAY 12

DEVOTIONAL

Have you ever experienced love and compassion from someone right when you needed it? Have you laughed or rejoiced with friends or family when you wanted to celebrate something great? Or, have you ever had a friend cry with you in a time of great trial and grief? In Romans 12:15, God commands us, *"Rejoice with those who rejoice, weep with those who weep."* We are called to be the hands and feet of Jesus because his heart is filled with compassion for people. David exemplifies this truth in Psalm 30:11 when he says, *"You have turned for me my mourning into dancing; you have loosed my sackcloth and clothed me with gladness."* Let's spend time today encountering God's heart of mercy for his people and learn how we can better share the love we've been shown with others.

As children of God, we are called to community. We are called to step away from the path of selfish ambition and sacrifice our lives for others the way Jesus has for us. Often this sacrificial life requires simply being there for those God has placed in our lives in whatever capacity they need. Colossians 3:12-13 says, *"Put on then, as God's chosen ones, holy and beloved, compassionate hearts, kindness, humility,*

> *"Rejoice with those who rejoice,*
> *weep with those who weep."*
>
> **ROMANS 12:15**

meekness, and patience, bearing with one another and, if one has a complaint against another, forgiving each other; as the Lord has forgiven you, so you also must forgive." God calls us to clothe ourselves with his heart. He asks us to be ambassadors for him by sharing his love with others. Philippians 2:3 says, *"Do nothing from selfish ambition or conceit, but in humility count others more significant than yourselves."* Jesus counted our redemption more important than his own life and *"humbled himself by becoming obedient to the point of death, even death on a cross."* (Philippians 2:8). And he asks us to be like him.

So, how can you and I live our lives like Jesus? How can we better *"rejoice with those who rejoice [and] weep with those who weep?"* It all starts with encountering the heart of God ourselves. Only in seeing the incredible compassion and love God has for you will you be able to have his heart for others.

2 Corinthians 1:3-4 says, *"Blessed be the God and Father of our Lord Jesus Christ, the Father of mercies and God of all comfort, who comforts us in all our affliction, so that we may be able to comfort those who are in any affliction, with the comfort with which we ourselves are comforted by God."* We're meant to love others out of the overflow of God's love for us. He doesn't ask you to have compassion and mercy in your own strength. He knows those are gifts that come from the Spirit working in our lives. You and I can do nothing in and of ourselves. To truly share God's heart we need God's help, and that starts with simply spending time encountering God for who he is.

After being filled with the love of God, you must choose to humble yourself before others and step outside of your comfort zone to bless someone. Humility requires strength, courage, and the help of the Holy Spirit. The Spirit will always help you share God's love for someone. Follow his leading, ask him for his heart for people around you, and follow through with courage in love. If you will make it your goal to see God's heart proclaimed through your life, you will experience more joy and purpose than you can imagine. Being a person who gives their own life for the sake of others will fill you with more peace and passion than living for yourself could ever produce. Spend time encountering God's heart today, and walk in obedience to his command: *"Rejoice with those who rejoice, weep with those who weep."* If you do so, you will find yourself filled with the knowledge of God's love today and satisfied in knowing you proclaimed God's love through your life.

GUIDED PRAYER

1. Meditate on God's love for you. Ask God to show you how he feels about you in this very moment.

"Blessed be the God and Father of our Lord Jesus Christ, the Father of mercies and God of all comfort, who comforts us in all our affliction, so that we may be able to comfort those who are in any affliction, with the comfort with which we ourselves are comforted by God." 2 Corinthians 1:3-4

2. Now ask for God's heart for someone else today. Who needs you to rejoice with them? Who needs you to weep with them?

"Rejoice with those who rejoice, weep with those who weep." Romans 12:15

"A new commandment I give to you, that you love one another: just as I have loved you, you also are to love one another." John 13:34

3. Right now in your own heart, humble yourself before the person that God has shown you. Choose in your own heart to count them as more significant than yourself. And commit to share God's love with them in whatever way the Spirit leads you.

"Do nothing from selfish ambition or conceit, but in humility count others more significant than yourselves." Philippians 2:3

"Put on then, as God's chosen ones, holy and beloved, compassionate hearts, kindness, humility, meekness, and patience, bearing with one another and, if one has a complaint against another, forgiving each other; as the Lord has forgiven you, so you also must forgive." Colossians 3:12-13

Choose to love people today in whatever situation you find yourself. Whether you're driving, having a conversation, working, or just relaxing with someone, you can always count others as more significant than yourself. You can always show others God's love. And the more you encounter God's heart for yourself, the more natural sharing his love with others will become. Share in the joy of co-laboring with God to see his kingdom, founded on love, come to earth today. There is no better life we can live than one spent working with our heavenly Father.

Extended Reading: 2 Corinthians 1

65

Live in Harmony

DAY 13

DEVOTIONAL

Harmony in music is this beautiful, fleeting occurrence that most singers and musicians work their entire lives to continuously experience. It requires diligence, patience, humility, and unity between people pursuing the same goal of making beautiful music. And when musical harmony is achieved, it touches not only those singing or playing, but everyone listening as well. Living in harmony with one another in everyday life isn't too different than musical harmony. For most of us it's a target just as elusive and fleeting. But like musical harmony, it's worth fighting for. Like musical harmony, it produces joy and life in those who pursue it and touches those around them. All throughout the New Testament, we find exhortations to live life in unified, harmonious community. Scripture is clear that unity in the body is foundational to the Christian

"Live in harmony with one another."

ROMANS 12:16

life. So, let's look more deeply today at how we can grow in unity and open our hearts to the Spirit's work to fill us with the desire and ability to pursue harmony with one another. Romans 12:16-20 says:

Live in harmony with one another. Do not be haughty, but associate with the lowly. Never be wise in your own sight. Repay no one evil for evil, but give thought to do what is honorable in the sight of all. If possible, so far as it depends on you, live peaceably with all. Beloved, never avenge yourselves, but leave it to the wrath of God, for it is written, "Vengeance is mine, I will repay, says the Lord." To the contrary, "if your enemy is hungry, feed him; if he is thirsty, give him something to drink; for by so doing you will heap burning coals on his head."

Not only does Paul offer us the important exhortation to live in harmony, but he also provides practical ways to achieve harmony. Romans 12 teaches us that harmony requires humility, grace, the pursuit of peace, not fighting for our own justice, and blessing those who hurt us. What would our communities, churches, and families look like if we all committed ourselves to these virtues? What would your relationships look like if you strived to obey these commands? God doesn't ask you and me to pursue these virtues; he commands us. It is a command because God knows that pursuing a life lived in harmony with one another will lead us to the abundance of joy, peace, and purpose we are created to experience. As our good Father, he wants his children to experience the peace that can only come from living in harmony with one another.

Not only do unity and harmony provide a better life for all involved, but they also glorify Jesus. Romans 15:5-6 says, *"May the God of endurance and encouragement grant you to live in such harmony with one another, in accord with Christ Jesus, that together you may with one voice glorify the God and Father of our Lord Jesus Christ."* When we love each other well and offer grace and forgiveness, we demonstrate Christ's power to change hearts to the world. When we live in harmony together, we worship with our lives in one beautiful, unified voice. The power of the gospel is that God will always love us in our pride and transgressions, but he doesn't intend to leave us there. God works in the hearts of his people, knitting them together in harmony like a beautiful tapestry of transformed lives. You and I are written into the pages of God's beautiful narrative. We have an important place in his eternal story of redemption. Spend time in God's presence today allowing him to fill you with the desire and ability to pursue harmony with others. Pursue unity with the people God's placed in your life. And experience transformation in your relationships as God works through you to produce unity and joy.

GUIDED PRAYER

1. Meditate on God's command to live in harmony with others.

"Live in harmony with one another. Do not be haughty, but associate with the lowly. Never be wise in your own sight. Repay no one evil for evil, but give thought to do what is honorable in the sight of all. If possible, so far as it depends on you, live peaceably with all. Beloved, never avenge yourselves, but leave it to the wrath of God, for it is written, 'Vengeance is mine, I will repay, says the Lord.' To the contrary, 'if your enemy is hungry, feed him; if he is thirsty, give him something to drink; for by so doing you will heap burning coals on his head.'" Romans 12:16-20

"That there may be no division in the body, but that the members may have the same care for one another. If one member suffers, all suffer together; if one member is honored, all rejoice together. Now you are the body of Christ and individually members of it." 1 Corinthians 12:25-27

2. Humble yourself and ask the Spirit to mold and shape you into a person who lives out the virtues of Romans 12.

"Complete my joy by being of the same mind, having the same love, being in full accord and of one mind." Philippians 2:2

"Finally, all of you, have unity of mind, sympathy, brotherly love, a tender heart, and a humble mind." 1 Peter 3:8

3. Now ask the Spirit for specific ways you can pursue harmony with others. Whom could you invite over for a meal to hear their story? Whom can you bless who has hurt you in the past? Whom could you associate yourself with that the world deems "lowly?" How can you honor that person you always seem to disagree with?

"And above all these put on love, which binds everything together in perfect harmony." Colossians 3:14

When you remove from yourself the burden of appearances, you will experience a joy and peace that cannot be found in any other lifestyle than humility. Caring what people think is exhausting! Climbing the ladder in your work, society, or relationships will never lead you to more satisfaction. There will always be another step to take, always another person to surpass. Choose to pursue harmony, unity, and love with those around you. Count them as more significant than yourself. If you will live your life in the pursuit of glorifying God instead of yourself, you will gain more satisfaction in this life than 10,000 lifetimes lived selfishly could produce.

Extended Reading: 1 Corinthians 12:12-31

Overcome Evil with Good

DAY 14

DEVOTIONAL

The world is filled with the destruction that sin and separation from God has caused. All around us are signs of the enemy's hand working tirelessly to keep God's children from the abundant life our Father longs to give. Even when looking at the state of the church, you see lives still impacted by either their own sin or the sin of others. Reflect for a minute on your own life. What are your struggles? What are the struggles you see in the lives of other believers around you? What about the world around you?

The last command God gives us in the Romans 12 passage we've been studying this week says, *"Do not be overcome by evil, but overcome evil with good"* (Romans 12:21). The idea of overcoming the world is a consistent concept throughout the entire New Testament. Scripture is clear that through the death of Christ we've been given the power and authority to overcome the work of the enemy in our own lives and lead others to freedom. Revelation 12:11 says, *"And they have conquered him by the blood of the Lamb and by the word of their*

> *"Do not be overcome by evil,
> but overcome evil with good."*
>
> **ROMANS 12:21**

testimony, for they loved not their lives even unto death." Conquering the enemy is our destiny as God's people. In Matthew 10:6-8 Jesus says, *"But go rather to the lost sheep of the house of Israel. And proclaim as you go, saying, 'The kingdom of heaven is at hand.' Heal the sick, raise the dead, cleanse lepers, cast out demons. You received without paying; give without pay."*

God gives us an important piece of his battle plan for the war against evil in Romans 12: we are to triumph over our enemy with good as our weapon. God doesn't fight evil with evil; he fights evil with love. It's the love of God that will lead you to victory over the enemy in your own life, and it's God's love that will be the weapon you use to lead other people to victory as well. God's goodness will draw you out of pursuing the world and lead you to victory as Revelation 12:11 says, *"They loved not their own lives even unto death."* And it is God's goodness that anoints you to *"heal the sick, raise the dead, cleanse lepers"* and *"cast out demons"* as Matthew 10 says. The goodness of God will always be more powerful than the enemy. His love will always triumph over the power of sin.

So, how can you *"overcome evil with good"* in your own life? James 4:7 says, *"Submit yourselves therefore to God. Resist the devil, and he will flee from you."* Because of the authority of your heavenly Father, when you put up a fight with the enemy, you will win. He will flee from you. That's God's promise to you. You have victory over the enemy in Christ because *"he who is in you is greater than he who is in the world"* (1 John 4:4). Greater is the Spirit who lives inside of you than the enemy who wages war against you. Finally, Galatians 5:1 says, *"For freedom Christ has set us free; stand firm therefore, and do not submit again to a yoke of slavery."*

Christ has set you free from bondage to the world. But you are free to choose who you submit yourself to. Experiencing consistent victory requires you to submit yourself to God and not to the world. You have to wake up and choose to live every day for God. You have to choose being successful in God's eyes instead of society's. You have to choose to live your life in light of eternity. But God promises if you will simply make that choice, he will lead you to victory over sin and its destructive effects and anoint you to help others do the same. In choosing God, you will discover the incredible life he has in store for those *"who love God"* and *"are called according to his purpose"* (Romans 8:28). Choose God today, and overcome evil with the goodness of restored relationship with your heavenly Father.

FAITH

GUIDED PRAYER

1. Meditate on God's promise to you of victory over the enemy.

"And they have conquered him by the blood of the Lamb and by the word of their testimony, for they loved not their lives even unto death." Revelation 12:11

"Little children, you are from God and have overcome them, for he who is in you is greater than he who is in the world." 1 John 4:4

2. Reflect on the areas of your life in which you need to overcome your enemy. Where do you struggle with sin? Where do you need victory today?

3. Now renew your mind to the truth of God's word while focusing on that area. Use God's truth as the sword to defeat the lies of your enemy.

"For freedom Christ has set us free; stand firm therefore, and do not submit again to a yoke of slavery." Galatians 5:1

"Submit yourselves therefore to God. Resist the devil, and he will flee from you." James 4:7

"Do not be conformed to this world, but be transformed by the renewal of your mind, that by testing you may discern what is the will of God, what is good and acceptable and perfect." Romans 12:2

Overcoming sin is a daily battle. But it is a battle that's already won. Experiencing the victory available to you will happen as you spend time with God every day meditating on his word and experiencing his goodness. Choose to place spending time with him above every other priority, and you will walk in victory over your enemy.

Extended Reading: Romans 12

DAYS 15 - 21

Encountering God

03

"Where shall I go from your Spirit? Or where shall I flee from your presence? If I ascend to heaven, you are there! If I make my bed in Sheol, you are there!" Psalm 139:7-8

WEEKLY OVERVIEW

Having consistent and transformational encounters with God while on earth is meant to be foundational to a life of faith. Our God has not left us. Through the sacrifice of Jesus, we've been filled with the very Spirit of God who longs to reveal to us daily the nearness and love of our heavenly Father. We are never alone. There is nowhere we can flee from the presence of our God. May this week be filled with transformational encounters with the living God as we learn what it is to seek the face of the one who has formed us, knows us, and loves us unconditionally.

Encountering God through Faith

DAY 15

DEVOTIONAL

By faith we come into the throne room of God and have an authentic, transformational encounter with our Creator. By faith we accept the free gift of eternal salvation. By faith we believe we will one day live in heaven with our Father. And it's by faith that we seek the fullness of relationship available to us on earth.

"And without faith it is impossible to please him, for whoever would draw near to God must believe that he exists and that he rewards those who seek him."

HEBREWS 11:6

Hebrews 11:6 says, *"And without faith it is impossible to please him, for whoever would draw near to God must believe that he exists and that he rewards those who seek him."* The Lord longs to reward your seeking him with an abundance of his presence. You can have consistent, transformational encounters with God. But in order to seek God, you must take him at his word. You must believe that he will reward you out of his good pleasure when you come to him with faith.

As we learned in prior weeks, Romans 10:17 says, *"So faith comes from hearing, and hearing through the word of Christ."* Faith is simply a response to God's promises and faithfulness. We can have faith because our God has proven himself wholly faithful. When he says in Revelation 3:20, *"Behold, I stand at the door and knock. If anyone hears my voice and opens the door, I will come in to him and eat with him, and he with me,"* he is making a foundational promise to you.

The Lord knocks on the door of your heart and longs to meet with you. He is asking you to have the faith to make space in your life, open your heart to him as an act of trust, and meet with him. His presence is fully available to you here. The veil separating us and the presence of God was torn by the power of Jesus' sacrifice.

Hebrews 10:22 says, *"Let us draw near with a true heart in full assurance of faith, with our hearts sprinkled clean from an evil conscience and our bodies washed with pure water."* I pray that your heart would be filled with the assurance that comes from faith in response to God's faithfulness. I pray that you would passionately pursue consistent encounters with your loving heavenly Father. I pray that today your faith will be rewarded with the powerful presence of the living God. And I pray that your life will forever be changed in light of how loving and near your Father is to you.

GUIDED PRAYER

1. Meditate on the importance of drawing near to God in faith.

"And without faith it is impossible to please him, for whoever would draw near to God must believe that he exists and that he rewards those who seek him." Hebrews 11:6

"And whatever you ask in prayer, you will receive, if you have faith." Matthew 21:22

2. Come before the throne of your God in faith that he will shepherd you into an encounter with his love.

"Let us draw near with a true heart in full assurance of faith, with our hearts sprinkled clean from an evil conscience and our bodies washed with pure water." Hebrews 10:22

"Behold, I stand at the door and knock. If anyone hears my voice and opens the door, I will come in to him and eat with him, and he with me." Revelation 3:20

3. Rest in the presence of your heavenly Father. Allow his love to lay a foundation of grace, joy, peace, and purpose in your heart.

"You will seek me and find me, when you seek me with all your heart." Jeremiah 29:13

May Psalm 139:7-12 fill your heart with faith to experience the nearness of your Father:

Where shall I go from your Spirit? Or where shall I flee from your presence? If I ascend to heaven, you are there! If I make my bed in Sheol, you are there! If I take the wings of the morning and dwell in the uttermost parts of the sea, even there your hand shall lead me, and your right hand shall hold me. If I say, "Surely the darkness shall cover me, and the light about me be night," even the darkness is not dark to you; the night is bright as the day, for darkness is as light with you.

Extended Reading: Psalm 139

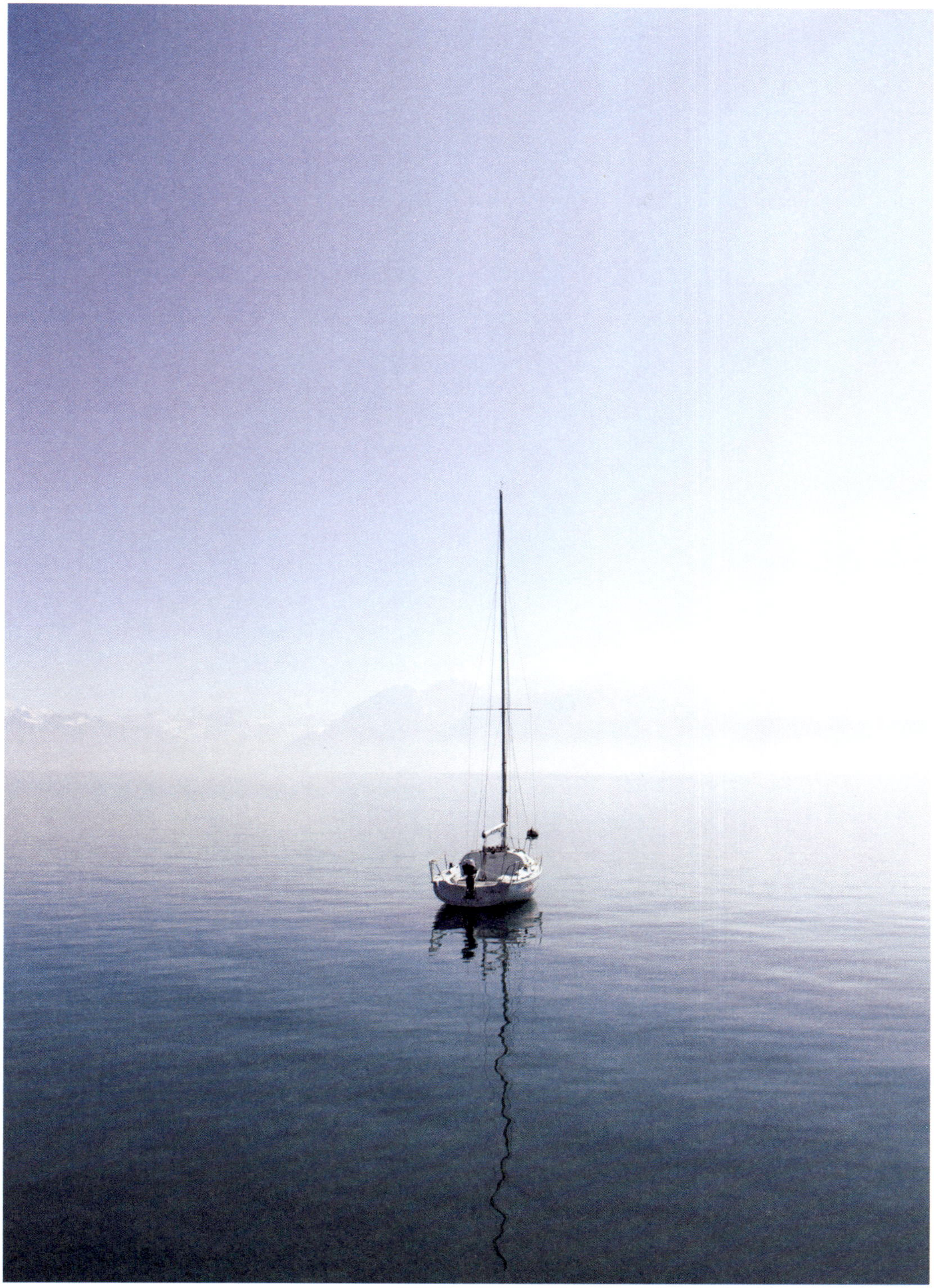

Encountering God through Prayer

DAY 16

DEVOTIONAL

Through prayer we have access to deep encounters with the heart and mind of our heavenly Father. Jeremiah 33:3 says, *"Call to me and I will answer you, and will tell you great and hidden things that you have not known."* God longs for us to call to him as our source of life, wisdom, guidance, and truth. He longs to answer our calls by shepherding us into a lifestyle of continually

*"Call to me and I will answer you,
and will tell you great and hidden
things that you have not known."*

JEREMIAH 33:3

seeking and receiving revelation from his word and Spirit. But in order for us to truly engage with God in prayer, we must learn what it means to listen.

Mother Teresa said, *"Prayer is not asking. Prayer is putting oneself in the hands of God, at His disposition, and listening to His voice in the depth of our hearts."* I find that we do not pray incorrectly as believers from a lack of earnest desire for God, but rather from a lack of knowledge and past experience. Do you know and believe that you can truly put yourself in the hands of your heavenly Father and listen to his voice as Mother Teresa did? Do you know that your Creator longs to open your eyes and heart to receive the knowledge of his love, will, and divine nature?

Taking time to listen to God in prayer is at the very core of Christian spirituality. It is a skill of the highest value that is only learned by patience, repetition, and faith. You can hear God because he wants to talk to you. You have no less inherent ability to hear God than me, Mother Teresa, or any of the disciples. Those who hear God are simply those who make space and seek out his voice.

Psalm 46:10 says, *"Be still, and know that I am God. I will be exalted among the nations, I will be exalted in the earth!"* In stillness we grow in our knowledge of who God truly is. God longs to make us a people who know him the way you know your family and friends. He longs to make us a people who live, think, and work out of true encounters with him. And learning to encounter God throughout your daily life starts with getting alone in the secret place, quieting your heart, and growing in your knowledge of God. Jesus taught us in Matthew 6:5-6:

And when you pray, you must not be like the hypocrites. For they love to stand and pray in the synagogues and at the street corners, that they may be seen by others. Truly, I say to you, they have received their reward. But when you pray, go into your room and shut the door and pray to your Father who is in secret. And your Father who sees in secret will reward you.

May you seek and find the knowledge of your heavenly Father today as you enter into the secret place, quiet your heart, and listen to him in guided prayer.

GUIDED PRAYER

1. Meditate on the importance of listening to your heavenly Father in prayer. Allow Scripture to stir up your faith and desire to know your Creator by being still, opening your heart, and listening.

"Be still, and know that I am God. I will be exalted among the nations, I will be exalted in the earth!" Psalm 46:10

"My son, if you receive my words and treasure up my commandments with you, making your ear attentive to wisdom and inclining your heart to understanding; yes, if you call out for insight and raise your voice for understanding, if you seek it like silver and search for it as for hidden treasures, then you will understand the fear of the Lord and find the knowledge of God." Proverbs 2:1-5

"Behold, I stand at the door and knock. If anyone hears my voice and opens the door, I will come in to him and eat with him, and he with me." Revelation 3:20

2. Ask the Lord to reveal himself to you in the secret place today. Ask him to shepherd you into an encounter with him that you might grow in your knowledge of his heart.

"But grow in the grace and knowledge of our Lord and Savior Jesus Christ. To him be the glory both now and to the day of eternity. Amen." 2 Peter 3:18

3. Take time to simply listen to God. He knows what you need even before you ask him for it. He will speak to you exactly what you need to hear. Pay attention to the way you feel as you quiet your heart. Pay attention to thoughts and ideas that he places in your heart. Pay attention to any desires that shift.

"Call to me and I will answer you, and will tell you great and hidden things that you have not known." Jeremiah 33:3

Brother Lawrence said, "There is not in the world a kind of life more sweet and delightful than that of a continual conversation with God." Meeting with God consistently is the foundation of everything God desires to give you in this life. All of the abundant life stems from a place of intimate and continuous encounters with your heavenly Father. May your ears and heart be opened to receiving the knowledge of your Father's love, grace, and purpose for your life. May you experience to greater levels the joy of intimacy with the God of love. And may your heart come alive in the stillness of meeting with the God who dwells in all of eternity.

Extended Reading: Psalm 42

Encountering God through Thanksgiving

DAY 17

DEVOTIONAL

Thanksgiving is a gift given to us by the good and loving nature of our heavenly Father. In and out of every season of life, we have a reason to give thanks because we serve a wholly faithful, good, and loving God. We serve the only King who would lay down his life for his unworthy, rebellious servants. We serve a God perfectly worthy of all the thanksgiving and praise we could possibly give.

In using the incredible gift of thanksgiving, we remind ourselves of how truly good our Father is. In thanksgiving, we experience the joy of a proper perspective and have

*"Enter his gates with thanksgiving,
and his courts with praise! Give thanks
to him; bless his name!"*

PSALM 100:4

our hearts stirred by the renewing of our minds. Psalm 100:4 says, *"Enter his gates with thanksgiving, and his courts with praise! Give thanks to him; bless his name!"* When we come before God with thanksgiving, we seek the face of our Father while grounding ourselves firmly in the truth of his perfect nature. When we begin our days, prayers, worship, reading, and fellowship with a heart of thanksgiving, we live out of a place of faith and reality found in the kingdom of God come to earth.

Our God is bigger and better than our circumstances, fears, wounds, misconceptions, and past failures. There is security and joy in declaring the goodness, kindness, loving, and eternal nature of our Father. We dictate the emotions we feel by what we choose to dwell on and believe. Our minds are the battleground for our emotions, actions, and desire to dwell in communion with our good God.

Ephesians 5:20 says we are to be *"giving thanks always and for everything to God the Father in the name of our Lord Jesus Christ."* And Psalm 92:1-5 says:

It is good to give thanks to the Lord, to sing praises to your name, O Most High; to declare your steadfast love in the morning, and your faithfulness by night, to the music of the lute and the harp, to the melody of the lyre. For you, O Lord, have made me glad by your work; at the works of your hands I sing for joy. How great are your works, O Lord! Your thoughts are very deep!

Our hearts become glad when we offer continual thanksgiving. Five minutes of thanksgiving and praise has the power to change the direction of each day. It has the power to stir our hearts and make us open to and aware of God's will for us in every situation. It fills us with an atmosphere of joy and of the Spirit. And it can greatly assist us in choosing the life of communion with the Father over the pursuits of the world as temptations and situations arise. May you be empowered and filled with transcendent joy as you engage in continual thanksgiving.

Take time in guided prayer to practice thanksgiving and enjoy the fruits of a renewed mind and a heart filled with joy and truth.

GUIDED PRAYER

1. Meditate on the importance of thanksgiving. Allow Scripture to stir up your desire to offer thanksgiving in every season.

"Continue steadfastly in prayer, being watchful in it with thanksgiving." Colossians 4:2

"Bless the Lord, O my soul, and forget not all his benefits." Psalm 103:2

"Oh come, let us sing to the Lord; let us make a joyful noise to the rock of our salvation! Let us come into his presence with thanksgiving; let us make a joyful noise to him with songs of praise!" Psalm 95:1-2

2. Take time to give thanks to God. Think about how he sent Jesus to die for you. Think about how faithful he is and always will be. Think about how good heaven will be. Give thanks for any gift he's given you.

"I will praise the name of God with a song; I will magnify him with thanksgiving. This will please the Lord more than an ox or a bull with horns and hoofs." Psalm 69:30-31

"We give thanks to you, O God; we give thanks, for your name is near. We recount your wondrous deeds." Psalm 75:1

3. How do you feel after taking time to engage in thanksgiving? Have your concerns, desires, and perspectives shifted? Journal about the effects of thanksgiving on your heart and mind.

We are continually commanded by Scripture to remember the deeds of our God. When the world comes crashing down around us, it's hard sometimes to remember how faithful God has been and will be. It's easy to get so wrapped up in the fleeting cares and problems of this life and forget how perfect and never-ending the next life will be. Psalm 103:2 says, *"Bless the Lord, O my soul, and forget not all his benefits."* May you be quick to remember the benefits of restored relationship with your heavenly Father today as you take time to bless and thank the Lord for all the wonderful things he's given you.

Extended Reading: Deuteronomy 8

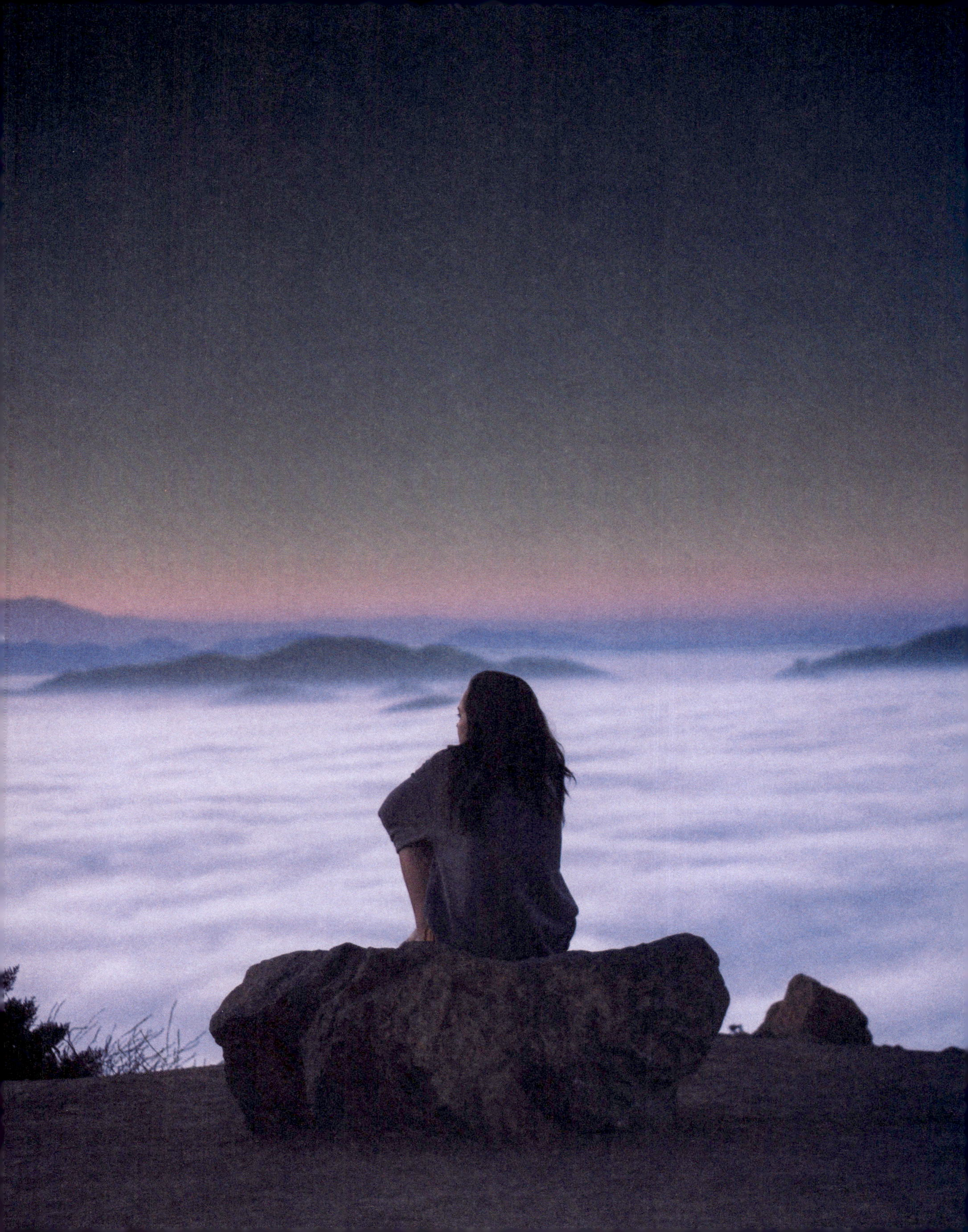

Encountering God through Worship

DAY 18

DEVOTIONAL

Jesus taught us in John 4:23, *"But the hour is coming, and is now here, when the true worshipers will worship the Father in spirit and truth, for the Father is seeking such people to worship him."* Your heavenly Father is seeking your worship. He longs for it. He so values your love and adoration that he would send his Son to die that the path to encountering him would be made available.

*"Ascribe to the Lord the glory due his name;
worship the Lord in the splendor of holiness."*

PSALM 29:2

You were first and foremost created to worship. You were created to receive the love of your Creator and in response give him your heart. You will never feel as whole as when your heart is connected to your Father's and you are giving and receiving love in worship. Colossians 3:14-17 says,

And above all these put on love, which binds everything together in perfect harmony. And let the peace of Christ rule in your hearts, to which indeed you were called in one body. And be thankful. Let the word of Christ dwell in you richly, teaching and admonishing one another in all wisdom, singing psalms and hymns and spiritual songs, with thankfulness in your hearts to God. And whatever you do, in word or deed, do everything in the name of the Lord Jesus, giving thanks to God the Father through him.

The Christian life is to be marked by heartfelt, genuine worship: worship filled with God's presence and nearness and that responds to a true encounter with the heart of God. If that type of worship is new to you, that's okay! If the idea of encountering God in worship is new to you, there is joy and grace at the place of new beginnings. Don't allow your past to dictate the possibilities of your future. Don't allow past experiences where worship might not have been filled with encountering Jesus make you believe that future times of worship won't be marked by intimacy and God's presence.

There is a new season of worship on the rise. Psalm 29:2 says, *"Ascribe to the Lord the glory due his name; worship the Lord in the splendor of holiness."* It's time for the people of God to worship in the *"splendor of holiness."* It's time for us to receive in faith our new position as children seated in the heavenly places with Jesus (Ephesians 2:6). It's time for us to seek encounters with our God that are unveiled and filled with God's presence (2 Corinthians 3:18). It's time to worship in both spirit and truth, with our hearts and our minds fully engaged and responsive.

Isaiah 12:5 says, *"Sing praises to the Lord, for he has done gloriously; let this be made known in all the earth."* May the world around you change as the result of your worship. May your declaration of God's goodness lead others into restored relationship with the Father. May your life be marked by intimacy and encounter with the living, active God of love who is nearer to you than you have ever imagined.

FAITH

GUIDED PRAYER

1. Meditate on the goodness of worshipping God in spirit and truth. Allow Scripture to fill you with a longing to encounter God through worship.

"But the hour is coming, and is now here, when the true worshipers will worship the Father in spirit and truth, for the Father is seeking such people to worship him." John 4:23

"Through him then let us continually offer up a sacrifice of praise to God, that is, the fruit of lips that acknowledge his name." Hebrews 13:15

"Ascribe to the Lord the glory due his name; worship the Lord in the splendor of holiness." Psalm 29:2

2. Ask the Lord to reveal to you his heart for intimacy in worship. Take time to seek out the desires of God that you might live to satisfy his longings for your worship.

"But from there you will seek the Lord your God and you will find him, if you search after him with all your heart and with all your soul." Deuteronomy 4:29

"The Lord is good to those who wait for him, to the soul who seeks him." Lamentations 3:25

3. Take some time and worship. Ask the Holy Spirit to help you praise from your heart. Engage your heart and mind with the lyrics of your favorite worship song. Worship and receive God's presence.

"Seek the Lord and his strength; seek his presence continually!" 1 Chronicles 16:11

"But for me it is good to be near God; I have made the Lord God my refuge, that I may tell of all your works." Psalm 73:28

Romans 12:1 says, *"I appeal to you therefore, brothers, by the mercies of God, to present your bodies as a living sacrifice, holy and acceptable to God, which is your spiritual worship."* We are created to worship through our lives. Every word, thought, action, and emotion can be done as worship if we will seek to commune with God in everything. God never leaves us; he never forsakes us (Deuteronomy 31:6). If we will keep our hearts open, we can live in the presence of our Creator, filled with the knowledge of his love and nearness in all we do. May we as God's people pursue with greater fervor what it is to truly worship.

Extended Reading: Psalm 33

Encountering God through Scripture

DAY 19

DEVOTIONAL

In Scripture, we have a perfect and direct avenue to powerful and transformational encounters with God. Jeremiah 15:16 says, *"Your words were found, and I ate them, and your words became to me a joy and the delight of my heart, for I am called by your name, O Lord, God of hosts."* In Scripture we find both our weakness and God's unfailing love portrayed through countless stories. God has spoken to us all we need in Scripture to both understand and pursue wholehearted, unveiled relationship with him.

"Your words were found, and I ate them, and your words became to me a joy and the delight of my heart, for I am called by your name, O Lord, God of hosts."

JEREMIAH 15:16

The very Spirit who authored the words of Scripture longs to use it to guide you and me into powerful encounters with our heavenly Father. I fear that many believers today are missing the intended meaning behind Scripture. The Bible is not God. It is designed to act as a guide to knowing its Author. It is designed to give us a desire and understanding about this God who is living, active, and near to us.

Isaiah 55:11 says, *"So shall my word be that goes out from my mouth; it shall not return to me empty, but it shall accomplish that which I purpose, and shall succeed in the thing for which I sent it."* God's purpose has always been restored relationship with his people. His goal is our hearts. And his word is powerful in accomplishing his purpose. Psalm 1:1-3 says,

Blessed is the man who walks not in the counsel of the wicked, nor stands in the way of sinners, nor sits in the seat of scoffers; but his delight is in the law of the Lord, and on his law he meditates day and night. He is like a tree planted by streams of water that yields its fruit in its season, and its leaf does not wither. In all that he does, he prospers.

The Lord longs to plant us by the streams of his presence. He longs for us to be a people that consistently and purposefully encounter his unending love. He longs for us to meditate on his laws that we might live according to his will and be blessed in all that we do. His heart is for us to know his love through his Spirit and word that we might live a truly abundant life marked by his unceasing faithfulness.

May we as fully loved children of the Most High God seek all that is available to us in Scripture. May we gain heart-knowledge about our Father as his word guides us into more consistent, true, and impactful encounters with him. May we be a people filled with the stories of God's redeeming love that we might live in response to the unchanging, active nature of our heavenly Father.

GUIDED PRAYER

1. Meditate on the importance of being a person who lives by the word of the Lord.

"Your words were found, and I ate them, and your words became to me a joy and the delight of my heart, for I am called by your name, O Lord, God of hosts." Jeremiah 15:16

"Blessed is the man who walks not in the counsel of the wicked, nor stands in the way of sinners, nor sits in the seat of scoffers; but his delight is in the law of the Lord, and on his law he meditates day and night. He is like a tree planted by streams of water that yields its fruit in its season, and its leaf does not wither. In all that he does, he prospers." Psalm 1:1-3

2. Ask the Holy Spirit to reveal truth you need to know through his word today. Ask him to guide you into a direct encounter with your heavenly Father as you open his word and read.

3. Take time to do the extended reading today. Allow the Holy Spirit to speak to your heart what you need to hear through the powerful words of Jesus.

"When the Spirit of truth comes, he will guide you into all the truth, for he will not speak on his own authority, but whatever he hears he will speak, and he will declare to you the things that are to come." John 16:13

Pray this prayer with me today:

Lord, make us a people who are endlessly hungry for your words of life. Make us a people who have so tasted and seen your goodness poured out in the pages of Scripture that we make time to feast on the bread of your word. Fill us with a longing for deeper, more consistent encounters with you that we would search the pages of Scripture for truths that will open our hearts to you more fully. May our lives be marked today by the fruit grown from the seed of your word.

Extended Reading: John 17

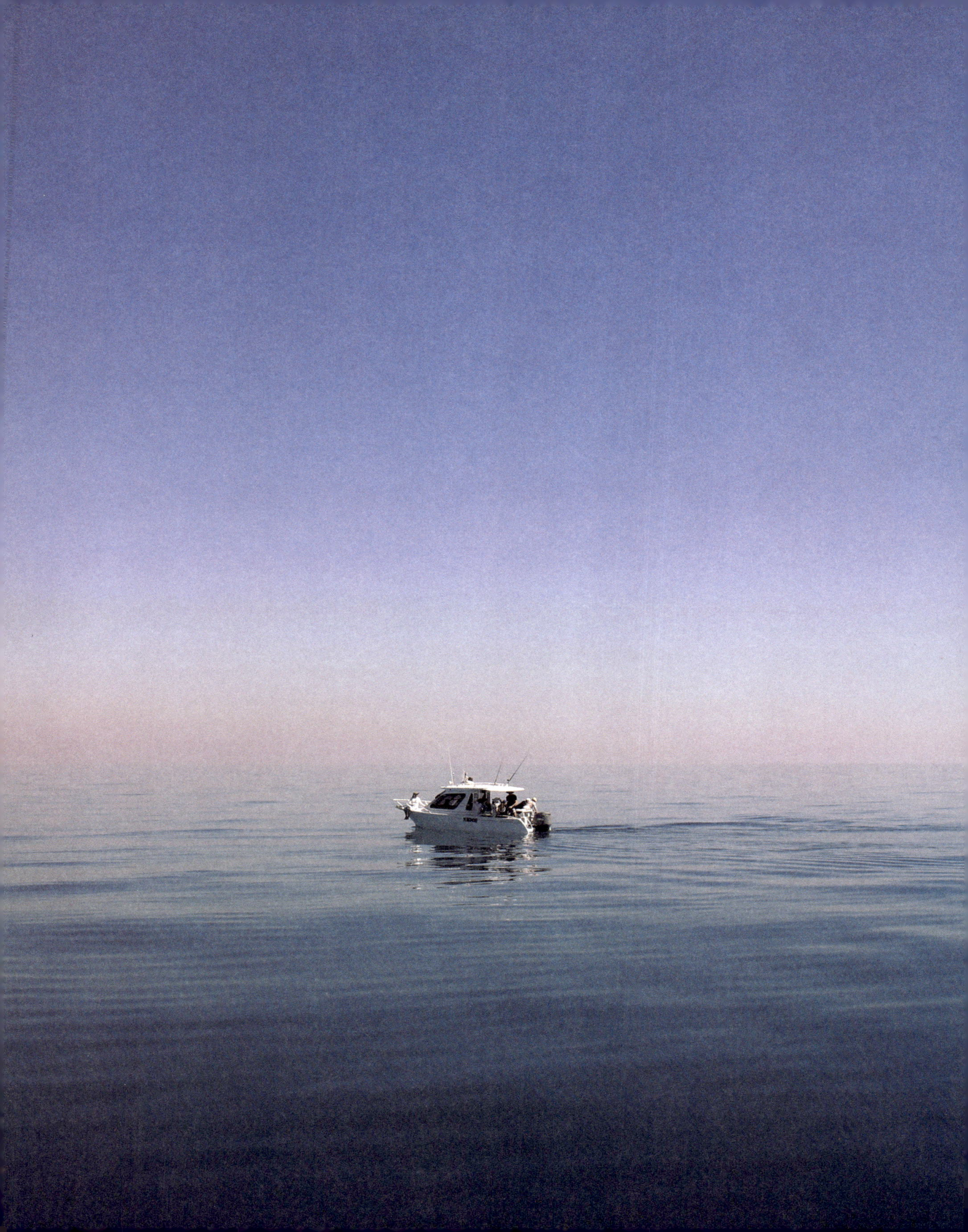

Encountering God through the Receiving of His Presence

DAY 20

DEVOTIONAL

God's presence has been made fully available to us by the sacrifice of Jesus, our pure and spotless Lamb. When we become Christians we are made totally new. 2 Corinthians 5:17 tells us, *"Therefore, if anyone is in Christ, he is a new creation. The old has passed away; behold, the new has come."* We are now able to fellowship with the presence of God in a closer and more intimate way than any people of God before the coming of Christ. We can now have God himself dwelling within us, his very Spirit fellowshipping with ours.

"Where shall I go from your Spirit? Or where shall I flee from your presence?"

PSALM 139:7

Ephesians 5:18 says, *"And do not get drunk with wine, for that is debauchery, but be filled with the Spirit."* To be filled with the Spirit is not a suggestion, it is a command. We as believers must continually be filled with the Spirit in order to access the fullness of relationship and life available to us on this earth. We need God's presence as sojourners on this earth. We need God's Spirit dwelling within us to live out the wonderful, life-giving commands of Scripture. We need God's Spirit to experience the fullness of God's presence available to us through the powerful sacrifice of Jesus.

You see, God's presence is already here. Psalm 139:7-12 says,

Where shall I go from your Spirit? Or where shall I flee from your presence? If I ascend to heaven, you are there! If I make my bed in Sheol, you are there! If I take the wings of the morning and dwell in the uttermost parts of the sea, even there your hand shall lead me, and your right hand shall hold me. If I say, "Surely the darkness shall cover me, and the light about me be night," even the darkness is not dark to you; the night is bright as the day, for darkness is as light with you.

You don't have to beg for an experience with God. He doesn't have to come from on high to the earth in order for you to encounter him. All that we have to do is quiet our hearts, align ourselves with the truth that he is here and available to us, and receive him. God never forces himself upon us. He never makes us have any part of him. But once we open our hearts to him and ask to encounter him, he is willing and able to fill us with his glorious presence. He is ready to make us aware of just how near to us he has always been—that he is closer than the very air we breathe.

Psalm 16:11 says, *"You make known to me the path of life; in your presence there is fullness of joy; at your right hand are pleasures forevermore."* May you come to know to greater levels the fullness of joy and pleasure available to you in the presence of your living and active God. May you grow in your awareness of the nearness and unconditional love of the Holy Spirit who dwells within you. May you receive God's presence throughout your day today and encounter the joy of the God who would lay down his own life simply for you to know him.

GUIDED PRAYER

1. Meditate on the nearness of God's presence. Allow Scripture to fill you with the desire and faith to encounter God today.

"Where shall I go from your Spirit? Or where shall I flee from your presence? If I ascend to heaven, you are there! If I make my bed in Sheol, you are there! If I take the wings of the morning and dwell in the uttermost parts of the sea, even there your hand shall lead me, and your right hand shall hold me. If I say, 'Surely the darkness shall cover me, and the light about me be night,' even the darkness is not dark to you; the night is bright as the day, for darkness is as light with you." Psalm 139:7-12

"And the disciples were filled with joy and with the Holy Spirit." Acts 13:52

2. Take a minute to quiet your heart and mind. Ask the Holy Spirit to help you receive God's presence. Take note of any desires you have as to whether you should sit quietly, worship, read, or pray. Follow whatever desire you have that will lead you into an encounter with God.

"Be still, and know that I am God. I will be exalted among the nations, I will be exalted in the earth!" Psalm 46:10

3. Open your heart and simply receive the presence of the God who already dwells within you. Ask the Holy Spirit to make his presence known to you. Take time to rest in an encounter with God's love and affection over you.

"All were made to drink of one Spirit." 1 Corinthians 12:13

"You make known to me the path of life; in your presence there is fullness of joy; at your right hand are pleasures forevermore." Psalm 16:11

In his book *The Furious Longing of God*, Brennan Manning describes a method of prayer that has helped me greatly in learning what it is to enter into God's presence. He says to pray this simple prayer: "Abba, I belong to you." As you inhale, pray the word "Abba." As you exhale, pray, "I belong to you." This idea of breathing and praying is an incredible depiction of what it is to receive the presence of God. He is nearer to us than the very breath that fills our lungs, and he will always respond to our desire to be filled with him. May this practice of God's presence fill you with a greater awareness of how real and near your God is to you today.

Extended Reading: Psalm 16

Encountering God through Others

DAY 21

DEVOTIONAL

One of the most impactful ways God reveals himself is through others. Jesus taught us in Matthew 18:19-20, *"Again I say to you, if two of you agree on earth about anything they ask, it will be done for them by my Father in heaven. For where two or three are gathered in my name, there am I among them."* We can learn aspects of God's heart through others that we simply can't learn alone. In relationship with others

> *"Again I say to you, if two of you agree on earth about anything they ask, it will be done for them by my Father in heaven. For where two or three are gathered in my name, there am I among them."*
>
> **MATTHEW 18:19-20**

we learn about God's heart for unity, grace, humility, and love in new and powerful ways. In fellowship we encounter people with various giftings, perspectives, and past experiences that are different than our own. And in community we discover God's heart to use others for the building up, healing, and sharpening of ourselves. James 5:13-16 says,

Is anyone among you suffering? Let him pray. Is anyone cheerful? Let him sing praise. Is anyone among you sick? Let him call for the elders of the church, and let them pray over him, anointing him with oil in the name of the Lord. And the prayer of faith will save the one who is sick, and the Lord will raise him up. And if he has committed sins, he will be forgiven. Therefore, confess your sins to one another and pray for one another, that you may be healed. The prayer of a righteous person has great power as it is working.

God longs for you to give yourself fully to the community around you. He longs to use you for the healing and building up of others. And he longs for you to embrace humility and receive help and sharpening from others around you.

Ephesians 4:16 says, *"From whom the whole body, joined and held together by every joint with which it is equipped, when each part is working properly, makes the body grow so that it builds itself up in love."* Investing in community gives you the opportunity to be used by God to be built up in love with a group of believers. It positions you to receive help from fellow believers who are pursuing Jesus. And it equips you to pursue freedom and life in areas where you might not have gotten victory without the help of others.

Pursue wholehearted community today, not because fellow believers are perfect, but because you, as an imperfect child of God, need help from fellow imperfect children to encounter the fullness of abundant life God intends for you. Have grace for others. Love when you are unloved. Help when no one else will. Build up the body that Jesus loves that the world might better know the loving and available God we serve.

GUIDED PRAYER

1. Meditate on the importance of investing in, and being invested in, by fellow believers.

"From whom the whole body, joined and held together by every joint with which it is equipped, when each part is working properly, makes the body grow so that it builds itself up in love." Ephesians 4:16

"Again I say to you, if two of you agree on earth about anything they ask, it will be done for them by my Father in heaven. For where two or three are gathered in my name, there am I among them." Matthew 18:19-20

2. Ask the Holy Spirit to show you whom you ought to invest in today and who he wants to use to invest in you. Ask God to help you humble yourself that you might love and show grace regardless of the faults of others.

3. Take some time and encourage a fellow believer. Ask God to show you his heart for that person and send them an encouragement from him. Ask God for a Scripture that he is speaking over that person. May you be used to build up another in love today.

I believe that the Lord has a few people for each of us that we are called to be totally open with. Oftentimes healing for our sin comes through confession and repentance to God and to fellow believers. When our sin is truly brought into the light in front of believers, we can better see it for what it is and gain help and accountability. May Ecclesiastes 4:9-12 encourage you today as you seek to develop much needed community with fellow believers:

Two are better than one, because they have a good reward for their toil. For if they fall, one will lift up his fellow. But woe to him who is alone when he falls and has not another to lift him up! Again, if two lie together, they keep warm, but how can one keep warm alone? And though a man might prevail against one who is alone, two will withstand him—a threefold cord is not quickly broken.

Extended Reading: Ephesians 4

DAYS 22 - 28

God's heart to meet with man

04

WEEK

"And behold, I am with you always, to the end of the age." Matthew 28:20

WEEKLY OVERVIEW

Throughout Scripture we see countless examples of God meeting with man and countless lives being transformed as the result. These examples are in Scripture to stir our faith and fill us with a desire to meet with our Creator. When we read about the life of David, we should be filled with a longing to live as he did, centered around meeting with our heavenly Father. When we read about Gideon or Moses, we should long to know our God as they did. When we read about Jesus coming down to us or his heart for the woman caught in adultery, we should respond by pursuing encounters with our Savior. And when we read of Pentecost and Jesus' second coming, we should seek out the fullness of God's presence available to us on this earth in preparation for the age that is to come. May your heart be filled with fresh faith and a wholehearted desire to pursue meeting with God this week.

God's Heart to Meet with David

DAY 22

DEVOTIONAL

The meetings between God and David shaped human history forever. David knew what it was to be in the presence of God. In fact, being in God's presence was his fuel, greatest joy, and source of courage. In Psalm 16:11 David writes, *"You make known to me the path of life; in your presence there is fullness of joy; at your right hand are pleasures forevermore."* And in verse 5 he writes, *"The Lord is my chosen portion and my cup; you hold my lot."* David was a man who consistently chose to meet with God over filling his days with the fleeting and unsatisfying things of the world. He centered his life around meeting with God, and it changed the history of not only his nation, but nations to come.

*"How lovely is your dwelling place, O Lord of hosts!
My soul longs, yes, faints for the courts of the Lord;
my heart and flesh sing for joy to the living God."*

PSALM 84:1-2

In 1 Samuel 17:34-37, we see a glimpse into the impact of David meeting with God early in his life. Scripture says,

But David said to Saul, "Your servant used to keep sheep for his father. And when there came a lion, or a bear, and took a lamb from the flock, I went after him and struck him and delivered it out of his mouth. And if he arose against me, I caught him by his beard and struck him and killed him. Your servant has struck down both lions and bears, and this uncircumcised Philistine shall be like one of them, for he has defied the armies of the living God." And David said, "The Lord who delivered me from the paw of the lion and from the paw of the bear will deliver me from the hand of this Philistine." And Saul said to David, "Go, and the Lord be with you!"

Out on the fields, David learned of God's power and desire for deliverance. He learned what it was to meet with God in the daily work of life. And he carried that knowledge with him into every battle, trial, and failure. We see it in Psalm 16:1-2 where David prays, *"Preserve me, O God, for in you I take refuge. I say to the Lord, 'You are my Lord; I have no good apart from you.'"*

King David, the greatest king that ever sat on the throne of Israel, claimed, *"I have no good apart from you."* David, about whom 1 Chronicles 29:28 says, *"Then he died at a good age, full of days, riches, and honor,"* claimed he had no good apart from the Lord. David knew that God's presence was the best part of life. He knew that meeting with his heavenly Father was far greater than any victory, possession, status, or honor. And it was for that reason that he lived a life full of the very thing he sought: the presence of the living God.

Your heavenly Father longs to meet with you as he did David. He loves you the same as he loved David. And through the powerful sacrifice of Jesus, you have even greater access to the heart of God. You have God, the Holy Spirit dwelling within you. Choose today to seek meeting with God above all else. Center your life around the presence of your heavenly Father the way David did. Live for transformational encounters with God and watch as the things of this world fall into proper place, providing you with transcendent peace, joy, and purpose in the midst of any circumstance.

GUIDED PRAYER

1. Meditate on David's longing for the presence of God. Allow Scripture to fill you with a desire to meet with your heavenly Father as David did.

"The Lord is my chosen portion and my cup; you hold my lot." Psalm 16:5

"You make known to me the path of life; in your presence there is fullness of joy; at your right hand are pleasures forevermore." Psalm 16:11

"Preserve me, O God, for in you I take refuge. I say to the Lord, 'You are my Lord; I have no good apart from you.'" Psalm 16:1-2

2. Allow these other Scriptures to fill you with faith to encounter the presence of God. The Holy Spirit is dwelling within you, ready to lead you into a transformational encounter with your heavenly Father.

"You will seek me and find me, when you seek me with all your heart." Jeremiah 29:13

"Where shall I go from your Spirit? Or where shall I flee from your presence?" Psalm 139:7

"Or do you not know that your body is a temple of the Holy Spirit within you, whom you have from God? You are not your own, for you were bought with a price." 1 Corinthians 6:19-20

3. Take time to meet with God. Ask him to reveal his nearness to you. Ask him to give you a passion for his presence like David had. Choose to center your life around the goodness of his nearness today.

"For a day in your courts is better than a thousand elsewhere. I would rather be a doorkeeper in the house of my God than dwell in the tents of wickedness." Psalm 84:10

How much better would our lives be if we simply chose to center them around meeting with the eternal, living, and active God of love? What would it be like to seek his counsel throughout our days? What would it be like to live wholly loved, liked, set free, and filled with his presence? Through Jesus, more has been made available to us than we know. We've been granted access to the fullness of life, love, and freedom. All that is required of us is to make space in our days and seek meeting with God above all else. May we as the bride of Christ choose to love our bridegroom above all else.

Extended Reading: 1 Samuel 17

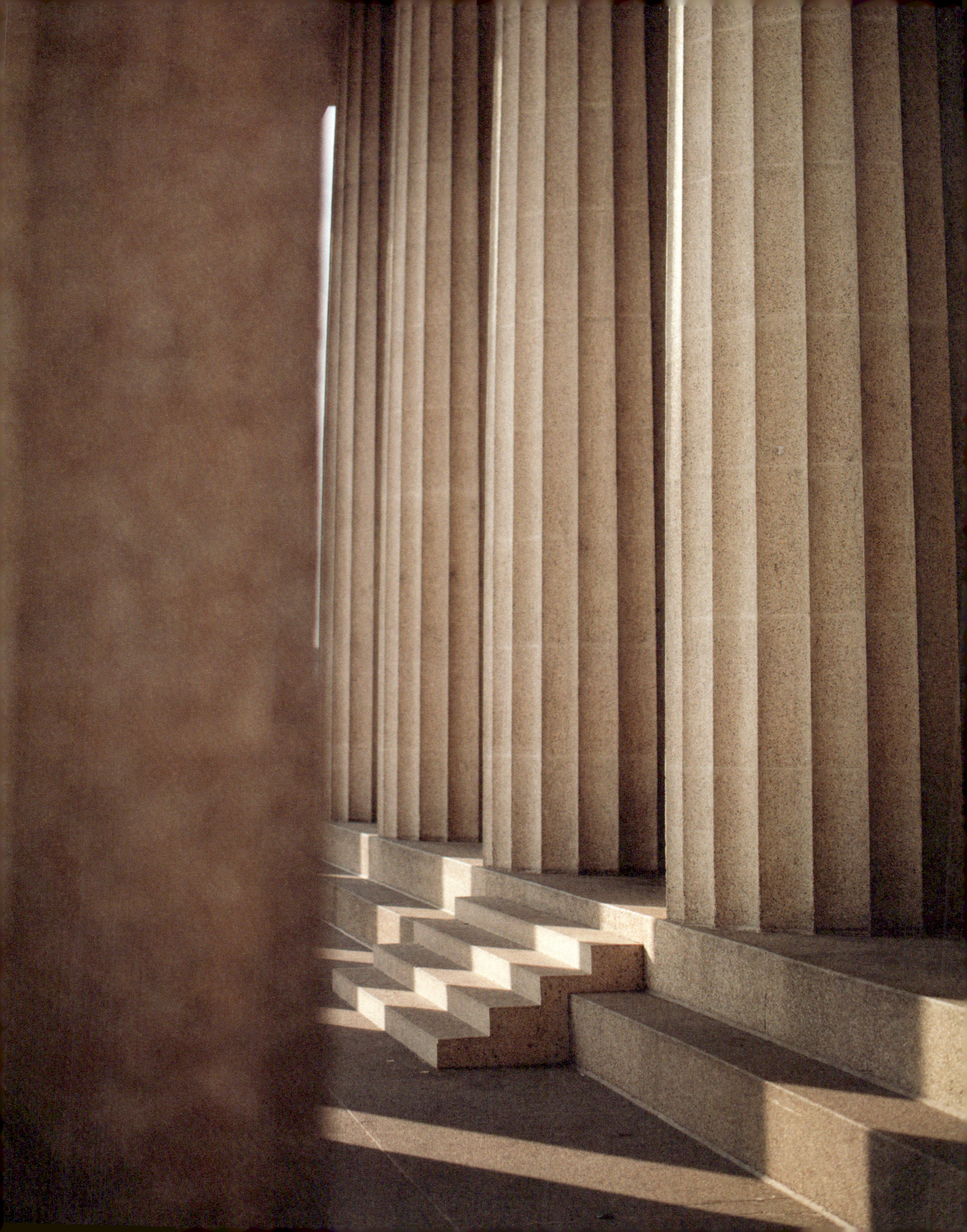

God's Heart to Meet with Gideon

DAY 23

DEVOTIONAL

The story of God meeting with Gideon ignites a fire of faith within me to be used by God to powerfully impact the earth. Gideon exemplifies the truth that God anoints all he appoints. He will perfectly equip and empower you to accomplish whatever task he has set before you.

"And the Lord said to him, 'But I will be with you, and you shall strike the Midianites as one man.'"

JUDGES 6:16

In Judges 6, an angel of the Lord approaches Gideon, who at the time was beating out wheat in a winepress to hide it from the oppressive Midianites. Scripture says, *"And the angel of the Lord appeared to him and said to him, 'The Lord is with you, O mighty man of valor'"* (Judges 6:12). Now, if an angel appeared to me and told me something, I'd like to think I would believe whatever he said. Not so with Gideon. Gideon immediately doubts the word of God. He responds to God's call to save Israel by saying, *"'Please, Lord, how can I save Israel? Behold, my clan is the weakest in Manasseh, and I am the least in my father's house.' And the Lord said to him, 'But I will be with you, and you shall strike the Midianites as one man'"* (Judges 6:15-16).

So great was Gideon's insecurity that he didn't trust a direct word from God. But God still responded to Gideon's doubt by meeting him at that place of insecurity and faithlessness and consistently speaking truth over him. Before Gideon even had a chance to doubt, God called him a *"mighty man of valor."* God knew Gideon's insecurities. He knew that his past and present works were anything but full of valor. But God called out the greatness he had placed in Gideon. In meeting with Gideon, he formed and fashioned him into a man full of faith and power.

In going into battle, the Lord took the vast number of men that were following Gideon, totaling thirty-two thousand, and stripped them down to three hundred. God took what might have been possible by the hands of Gideon and made it only possible by his great strength. And in response to God's faithfulness to meet with him, Gideon obeyed the Lord and confidently went into battle with three hundred men. Judges 7:22-23 tells us, *"When they blew the 300 trumpets, the Lord set every man's sword against his comrade and against all the army. And the army fled as far as Beth-shittah toward Zererah, as far as the border of Abel-meholah, by Tabbath. And the men of Israel were called out from Naphtali and from Asher and from all Manasseh, and they pursued after Midian."*

Gideon powerfully defeated an oppressive army vastly outnumbering his own because of the power of God working through him. God longs to fill you and empower you today. He longs to conquer the works of the enemy that oppress those he loves through you. Meet with God today. Allow him to call out the greatness he has placed within you. Allow him to guide you into battles only he could win that you might bring his kingdom to earth all around you. May you be filled with his love, grace, and power today as you open your heart and spend time communing with your heavenly Father.

FAITH

GUIDED PRAYER

1. Meditate on the powerful effect of God's heart to meet with Gideon. Allow the grace God had for Gideon to fill you with an understanding of God's grace toward you. Allow Scripture to stir up your heart and faith to meet with God.

"'Please, Lord, how can I save Israel? Behold, my clan is the weakest in Manasseh, and I am the least in my father's house.' And the Lord said to him, 'But I will be with you, and you shall strike the Midianites as one man.'" Judges 6:15-16

"Then Gideon said to God, 'If you will save Israel by my hand, as you have said, behold, I am laying a fleece of wool on the threshing floor. If there is dew on the fleece alone, and it is dry on all the ground, then I shall know that you will save Israel by my hand, as you have said.' And it was so. When he rose early next morning and squeezed the fleece, he wrung enough dew from the fleece to fill a bowl with water. Then Gideon said to God, 'Let not your anger burn against me; let me speak just once more. Please let me test just once more with the fleece. Please let it be dry on the fleece only, and on all the ground let there be dew.' And God did so that night; and it was dry on the fleece only, and on all the ground there was dew." Judges 6:36-40

"I can do all things through him who strengthens me." Philippians 4:13

2. What are the Midianites in your life? What does God want to conquer in and through you today?

3. Open your heart to the Lord and meet with him. Meditate on his nearness. Ask the Holy Spirit to reveal his presence to you.

"Behold, I stand at the door and knock. If anyone hears my voice and opens the door, I will come in to him and eat with him, and he with me." Revelation 3:20

"You will seek me and find me, when you seek me with all your heart." Jeremiah 29:13

May Romans 8:35 and 37-39 encourage you and fill you with faith to conquer all that would stand in the way of you and the abundant life Jesus died to give you:

Who shall separate us from the love of Christ? Shall tribulation, or distress, or persecution, or famine, or nakedness, or danger, or sword? . . . No, in all these things we are more than conquerors through him who loved us. For I am sure that neither death nor life, nor angels nor rulers, nor things present nor things to come, nor powers, nor height nor depth, nor anything else in all creation, will be able to separate us from the love of God in Christ Jesus our Lord.

Extended Reading: Judges 6-7

God's Heart to Meet with Moses

DAY 24

DEVOTIONAL

The story of Moses is one marked by powerful encounters with the presence of God. Moses was a man anointed by God to fulfill God's heart for his children to be free from captivity and safe under his lordship. From birth, Moses was divinely set apart to lead God's people back into right relationship with God. And this calling was fulfilled because of God's desire to consistently meet with Moses and show up through his life in miraculous ways. In looking at the life of Moses, two types of encounters with God stand out as especially transformative and illustrative of God's heart to meet with his people. As we look at these two examples of God meeting Moses, may Scripture fill your heart with a desire to meet with your heavenly Father as Moses did.

First, Exodus 3:1-6 gives us insight into the first real encounter Moses had with the Great I Am. Scripture says,

Now Moses was keeping the flock of his father-in-law, Jethro, the priest of Midian, and he led his flock to the west side of the wilderness and came to Horeb, the mountain of God. And the angel of the Lord appeared to him in a flame of fire out of the midst of a bush. He looked, and behold, the bush was burning, yet it was not consumed. And Moses said, "I will turn aside to see this great sight, why the bush is not burned." When the Lord saw that he turned aside to see, God called to him out of the bush, "Moses, Moses!" And he said, "Here I am." Then he said, "Do not come near; take your sandals off your

> *"Thus the Lord used to speak to Moses face to face, as a man speaks to his friend."*
>
> **EXODUS 33:11**

feet, for the place on which you are standing is holy ground." And he said, "I am the God of your father, the God of Abraham, the God of Isaac, and the God of Jacob." And Moses hid his face, for he was afraid to look at God.

In the story of the burning bush, we see God's grace and divine favor on the life of an undeserving man. Moses had fled the scene after murdering an Egyptian for assaulting a Hebrew man. For years he had been hiding in the desert, living outside of any real earthly impact. But God called Moses out of the wilderness into a life of deep, eternal impact.

Second, we see God's heart to consistently meet with Moses in the Tent of Meeting found in Exodus 33:7-11. Scripture says,

Now Moses used to take the tent and pitch it outside the camp, far off from the camp, and he called it the tent of meeting. And everyone who sought the Lord would go out to the tent of meeting, which was outside the camp. Whenever Moses went out to the tent, all the people would rise up, and each would stand at his tent door, and watch Moses until he had gone into the tent. When Moses entered the tent, the pillar of cloud would descend and stand at the entrance of the tent, and the Lord would speak with Moses. And when all the people saw the pillar of cloud standing at the entrance of the tent, all the people would rise up and worship, each at his tent door. Thus the Lord used to speak to Moses face to face, as a man speaks to his friend. When Moses turned again into the camp, his assistant Joshua the son of Nun, a young man, would not depart from the tent.

How incredible is the heart of our God that he would meet with Moses *"face to face, as a man speaks to his friend."* If God would meet with Moses, a man who has not been redeemed by the sacrifice of Jesus, how much more would he meet with you and me? If God would show grace to Moses, how much more available is grace to us who now have God himself dwelling within us!

You and I have access to relationship far greater than a face-to-face encounter like Moses had. We have God's Spirit within us fellowshipping with our Spirit. We never have to leave the burning bush or the Tent of Meeting. True restored relationship finds its source in continual, unending encounters with God's presence dwelling with us and upon us.

May you pursue the greater portion of relationship with your heavenly Father today. May your Spirit come alive as you grow in your awareness of God's Spirit. May you have powerful, transformative encounters with God's presence likened to that which Moses experienced.

GUIDED PRAYER

1. Meditate on God's desire to meet with Moses.
Allow Scripture to fill you with a longing to meet with God as Moses did.

"When the Lord saw that he turned aside to see, God called to him out of the bush, 'Moses, Moses!' And he said, 'Here I am.' Then he said, 'Do not come near; take your sandals off your feet, for the place on which you are standing is holy ground.' And he said, 'I am the God of your father, the God of Abraham, the God of Isaac, and the God of Jacob.' And Moses hid his face, for he was afraid to look at God." Exodus 3:4-6

"When Moses entered the tent, the pillar of cloud would descend and stand at the entrance of the tent, and the Lord would speak with Moses. And when all the people saw the pillar of cloud standing at the entrance of the tent, all the people would rise up and worship, each at his tent door. Thus the Lord used to speak to Moses face to face, as a man speaks to his friend. When Moses turned again into the camp, his assistant Joshua the son of Nun, a young man, would not depart from the tent." Exodus 33:9-11

2. Where can you make your tent of meeting?
Where and when can you consistently encounter the presence of God and meet with your heavenly Father face-to-face?

3. Take time to meet with God as Moses did.
Open your heart and ask the Holy Spirit to reveal his nearness.

"If you love me, you will keep my commandments. And I will ask the Father, and he will give you another Helper, to be with you forever, even the Spirit of truth, whom the world cannot receive, because it neither sees him nor knows him. You know him, for he dwells with you and will be in you." John 14:15-17

Having a consistent time and place to meet with God allows us to develop a rhythm by which we grow in experiencing God's presence. To have our own Tent of Meeting is vital to Christian spirituality. Choose a place and time that won't get disrupted and will help you center your life around meeting with your heavenly Father. These is absolutely nothing more important or pressing than seeing the face of God and being transformed by his love and nearness every day.

Extended Reading: Exodus 3

WEEK 4

125

DEVOTIONAL

There is no more powerful depiction of God's love for us than Jesus stepping off his throne to humble himself, take on flesh, and dwell among men. Jesus coming down to us perfectly demonstrated God's grace and desire to meet with man.

Imagine for a minute the sacrifice of Jesus. Prior to coming down to us, he was Spirit, like God the Father and the Holy Spirit. He dwelled everywhere in every point of time. He was in perfect communion with the Father and the Holy Spirit. Jesus gave up the very

> *"'Behold, the virgin shall conceive and bear a son, and they shall call his name Immanuel' (which means, God with us)."*
>
> **MATTHEW 1:23**

nature of his existence that we might walk in restored relationship with God. He sacrificed being Spirit that we might simply know God's love.

Jesus was the heart of God perfectly personified. In everything he did, he clearly displayed God's heart for mercy, grace, justice, redemption, and empowerment for his people. He is the center of all history. All of creation looks to him as King of kings and Lord of lords. Isaiah 9:6 tells us, *"For to us a child is born, to us a son is given; and the government shall be upon his shoulder, and his name shall be called Wonderful Counselor, Mighty God, Everlasting Father, Prince of Peace."*

We serve the only King who would lay down his own life for his undeserving, rebellious subjects. We serve the only God who would step down off his throne and humble himself before us, even to the point of death. We serve the God of perfect love who can do nothing that isn't completely drenched with his affection for us.

You can look at the life, death, and resurrection of Jesus and know without a shadow of a doubt that God longs to meet with you. If Jesus would come to earth that you might receive redemption and restored relationship with your heavenly Father, there is no doubt that he will meet you exactly where you are, right now. Jesus' sacrifice was so powerful that it set you free to live in true communion with God.

Ephesians 2:4-7 says,

But God, being rich in mercy, because of the great love with which he loved us, even when we were dead in our trespasses, made us alive together with Christ—by grace you have been saved— and raised us up with him and seated us with him in the heavenly places in Christ Jesus, so that in the coming ages he might show the immeasurable riches of his grace in kindness toward us in Christ Jesus.

May you discover what it truly means to be seated in the heavenly places with Christ. May you pursue all the fullness of relationship afforded to you by the powerful sacrifice of Jesus. May his coming to earth demonstrate its power in your life. Take time to fellowship with God today the way Jesus did. Walk as he walked. And experience today the fullness of life that only comes by meeting with your heavenly Father by his grace and love.

GUIDED PRAYER

1. Meditate on God's desire to meet with you as demonstrated by Jesus coming to earth.

"'Behold, the virgin shall conceive and bear a son, and they shall call his name Immanuel' (which means, God with us)." Matthew 1:23

"And the Word became flesh and dwelt among us, and we have seen his glory, glory as of the only Son from the Father, full of grace and truth." John 1:14

"Have this mind among yourselves, which is yours in Christ Jesus, who, though he was in the form of God, did not count equality with God a thing to be grasped, but emptied himself, by taking the form of a servant, being born in the likeness of men. And being found in human form, he humbled himself by becoming obedient to the point of death, even death on a cross." Philippians 2:5-8

2. Where do you have doubt about experiencing the presence of God? Where do you feel like it is impossible or difficult to encounter your heavenly Father?

"For God so loved the world, that he gave his only Son, that whoever believes in him should not perish but have eternal life." John 3:16

3. Align your perspective with the truth of Scripture. Allow Jesus' coming to fill you with faith and expectation to experience all that he came and died to give you. Take time to press into the heart of God and encounter the depths of his love today.

"But God, being rich in mercy, because of the great love with which he loved us, even when we were dead in our trespasses, made us alive together with Christ—by grace you have been saved— and raised us up with him and seated us with him in the heavenly places in Christ Jesus, so that in the coming ages he might show the immeasurable riches of his grace in kindness toward us in Christ Jesus." Ephesians 2:4-7

We as modern-day believers often grow content with so much less than what's available to us in Christ. We grow content with programs, sermons, worship, and Bible study that's void of God's presence. We believe that the Christian life is one solely marked by discipline and moral living rather than transformative encounters with the holiness of God. Pursue the greater things today. Press into the heart of your Creator that you might know how truly near he is. Seek him and discover the wealth of his presence and love that has been available to you all along. Instead of programs about him, may your life be marked by meeting directly with your good and loving Father.

Extended Reading: Philippians 2

129

DEVOTIONAL

The story of the woman caught in adultery is one the most powerful depictions of God's heart to meet man in the midst of sin and show grace. Scripture says,

Early in the morning he came again to the temple. All the people came to him, and he sat down and taught them. The scribes and the Pharisees brought a woman who had been caught in adultery, and placing her in the midst they said to him, "Teacher, this woman has been caught in the act of adultery. Now in the Law Moses commanded us to stone such women. So what do you say?" This they said to test him, that they might have some charge to bring against him. Jesus bent down and wrote with his finger on the ground. And as they continued to ask him, he stood up and said to them, "Let him who is without sin among you be the first to throw a stone at her." And once more he bent down and wrote on the ground. But when they heard it, they went away one by one, beginning with the older ones, and Jesus was left alone with the woman standing before him. Jesus stood up and said to her, "Woman, where are they? Has no one condemned you?" She said, "No one, Lord." And Jesus said, "Neither do I condemn you; go, and from now on sin no more." John 8:2-11

When I find myself in the midst of sin, my first instinct is to run away from God. For some reason we seem to hold this belief that God is like us: that he loves us like we love ourselves. I assume he's even more ashamed of me than I am of myself. I assume he's distanced himself from me in my sin. I assume that he can't be near to me or that his grace surely isn't strong enough for my sin this time. But Jesus' actions when presented with the woman caught in adultery completely obliterate my worldly perceptions of his grace.

Imagine the fear this woman feels. Imagine the horrific embarrassment and shame she feels being caught in the act of terrible sin and dragged before Jesus, God incarnate. Put yourself in her position. Feel the piercing glares of onlookers. Try and hear the terrible judgements being hurled your way by these religious leaders.

Now imagine Jesus standing before you, drawing in the sand as he did that day. Imagine what he would say to you in your sin. He doesn't seem surprised. He doesn't seem worried. He doesn't even cast judgment on you. Instead, he shows you the fullness of grace for your sin.

God longs to cast away all the lies the accuser would speak to you. He longs to cause all the judgments you speak over yourself and that others have spoken over you to flee in light of his powerful grace. Jesus stands before you today with nail-pierced hands having fully paid the price for each one of your sins. He's ready to empower you to *"Go, and from now on sin no more"* by his love and grace. Receive his love today. Allow him to meet you in the midst of your sin. Run into his arms instead of away from him. And live empowered to experience the fullness of his presence and total freedom from sin.

GUIDED PRAYER

1. Meditate on God's heart to meet us in our sin as displayed through the woman caught in adultery.

"Early in the morning he came again to the temple. All the people came to him, and he sat down and taught them. The scribes and the Pharisees brought a woman who had been caught in adultery, and placing her in the midst they said to him, 'Teacher, this woman has been caught in the act of adultery. Now in the Law Moses commanded us to stone such women. So what do you say?' This they said to test him, that they might have some charge to bring against him. Jesus bent down and wrote with his finger on the ground. And as they continued to ask him, he stood up and said to them, 'Let him who is without sin among you be the first to throw a stone at her.' And once more he bent down and wrote on the ground. But when they heard it, they went away one by one, beginning with the older ones, and Jesus was left alone with the woman standing before him. Jesus stood up and said to her, 'Woman, where are they? Has no one condemned you?' She said, 'No one, Lord.' And Jesus said, 'Neither do I condemn you; go, and from now on sin no more.'" John 8:2-11

2. Where are you closing off your heart to God as the result of your sin? Where do you feel unloveable? Where have lies and accusations caused you to withdraw yourself from God rather than run to him?

"There is therefore now no condemnation for those who are in Christ Jesus." Romans 8:1

3. Take time to receive the grace, forgiveness, and love of your heavenly Father. Confess your sin to him and rest in his loving presence.

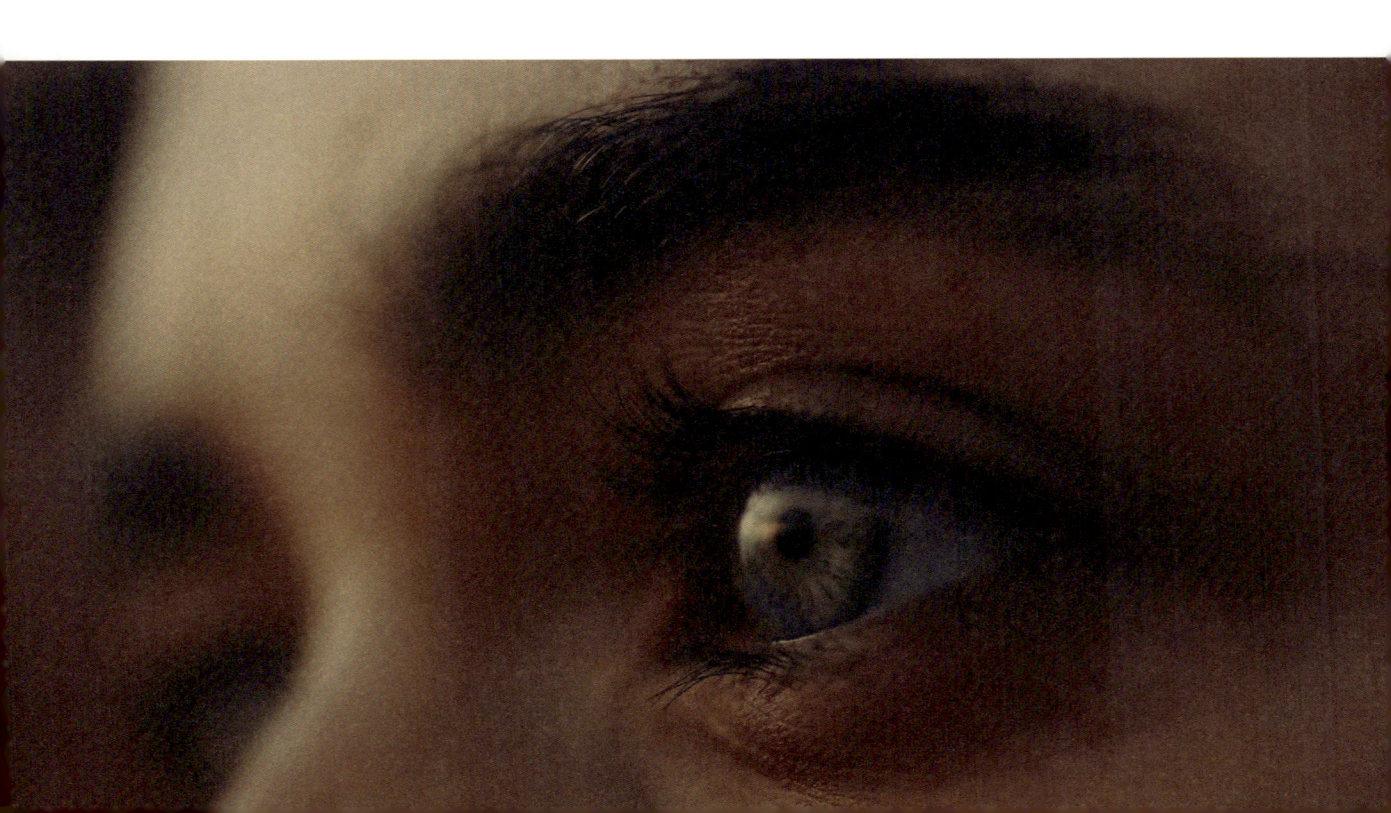

Be filled with the power of his grace that you might walk in freedom today.

"If we confess our sins, he is faithful and just to forgive us our sins and to cleanse us from all unrighteousness."
1 John 1:9

May 1 John 2:1-2 fill you with faith to run to Jesus with your sin rather than away from him in shame or judgment:

My little children, I am writing these things to you so that you may not sin. But if anyone does sin, we have an advocate with the Father, Jesus Christ the righteous. He is the propitiation for our sins, and not for ours only but also for the sins of the whole world.

Extended Reading: Romans 8

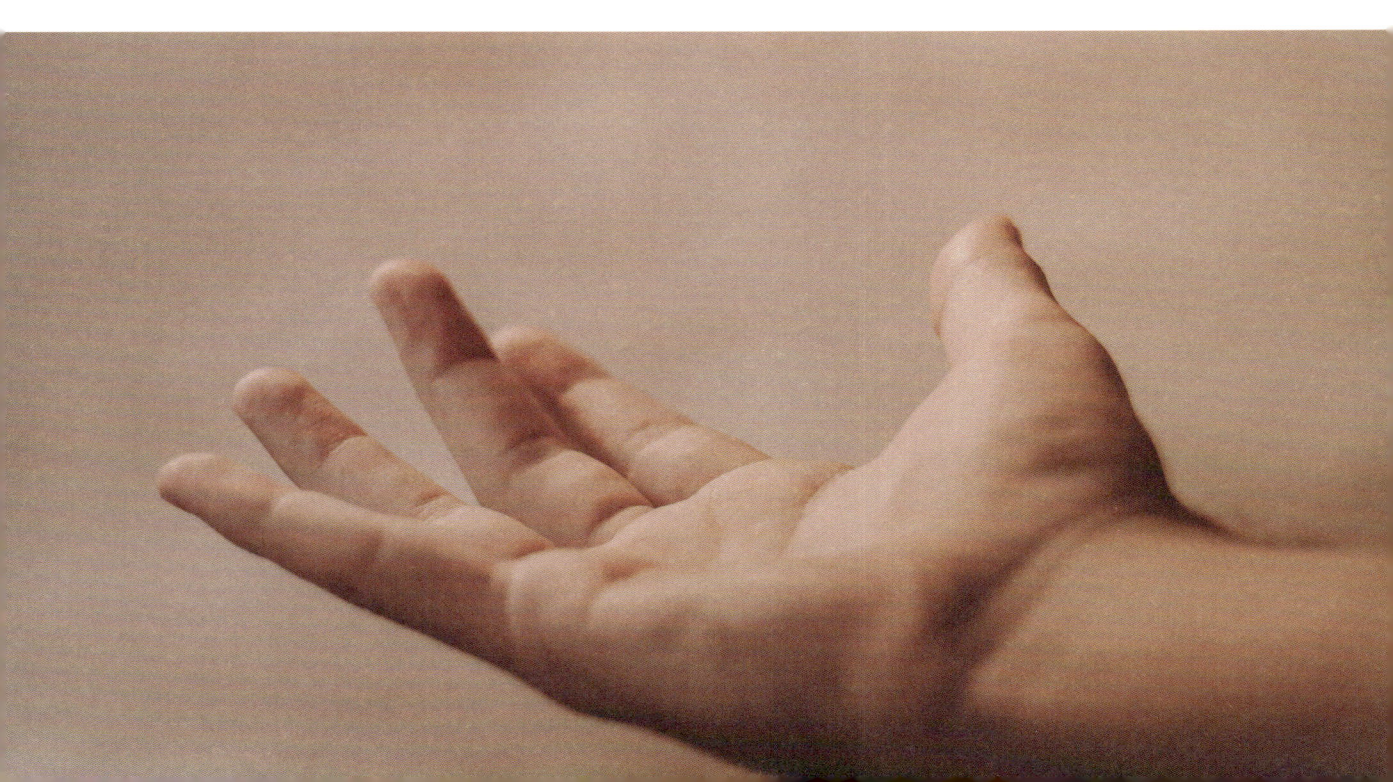

God's Heart to Meet with Man at Pentecost

DAY 27

SCRIPTURE

"When the day of Pentecost arrived, they were all together in one place. And suddenly there came from heaven a sound like a mighty rushing wind, and it filled the entire house where they were sitting. And divided tongues as of fire appeared to them and rested on each one of them. And they were all filled with the Holy Spirit and began to speak in other tongues as the Spirit gave them utterance." Acts 2:1-4

DEVOTIONAL

In the miraculous and powerful event of Pentecost, we see God's heart to not only dwell among us, but within us. We've been afforded more intimacy with God than we have fully grasped. The God of Pentecost dwells within us right now as believers, ready to equip us and empower us for a life of powerful impact and restored relationship. Acts 2:1-4 says,

When the day of Pentecost arrived, they were all together in one place. And suddenly there came from heaven a sound like a mighty rushing wind, and it filled the entire house where they were sitting. And divided tongues as of fire appeared to them and rested on each one of them. And they were all filled with the Holy Spirit and began to speak in other tongues as the Spirit gave them utterance.

Scripture tells us that although those in attendance spoke many different languages, all heard those filled with the Holy Spirit declaring *"in our own tongues the mighty works of God"* (Acts 2:11). And upon being filled with the Holy Spirit afresh, Peter begins to share the gospel with those present. Acts 2:41 tells us, *"Those who received his word were baptized, and there were added that day about three thousand souls."* Peter, who denied Jesus, begins his powerful, courageous ministry of sharing the gospel with all those who would listen after being empowered by the Holy Spirit.

Ephesians 5:18 tells us, *"And do not get drunk with wine, for that is debauchery, but be filled with the Spirit."* This passage is better translated, *"Be being filled with the Spirit."* The Holy Spirit is our gateway into the fullness of life available to us in Christ. He's the one who reveals to us the truth of Scripture. He's the one who speaks to our hearts from the mouth of God. He's the one who makes us aware of God's presence. And he's the one who empowers us to do the good works set before us before the foundation of the earth. Without relationship with the Holy Spirit, we will miss out on the incredible life afforded to us by the life, death, and resurrection of Jesus.

God wants to empower you to impact the earth the way the disciples did. His plan for you doesn't involve that which is fleeting and temporal. At the end of your life, will you look back and be thankful for the way you said yes to walking with the Holy Spirit, or will your life be filled with works that won't outlive you? Don't waste this life being satisfied with less than what is available to you. Choose today to be filled with the Holy Spirit again. Choose to pursue wholehearted relationship with him. And say yes to him at every decision that you might reveal to the world the wealth of relationship available to you in the Holy Spirit.

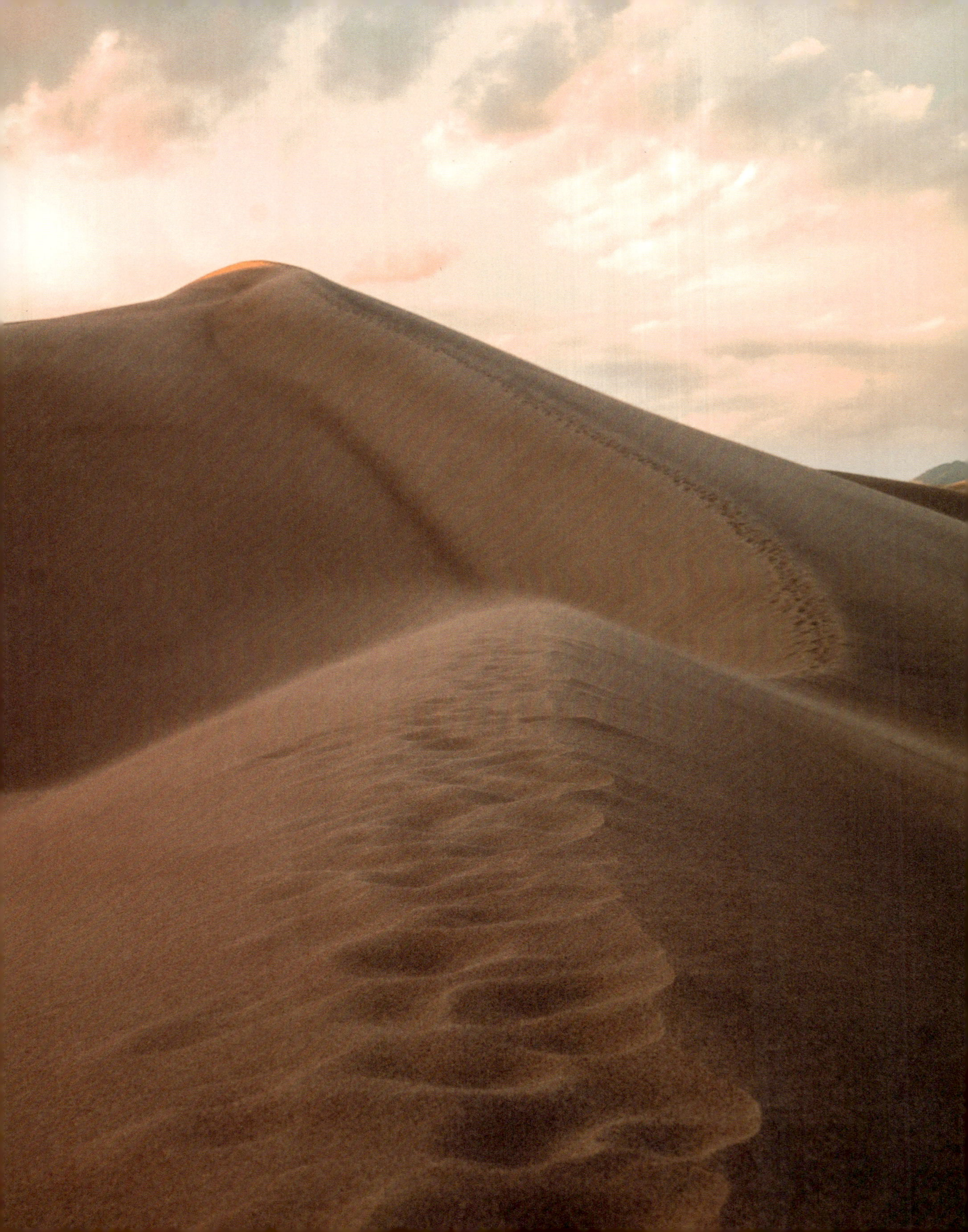

GUIDED PRAYER

1. Meditate on the importance of being filled with the Spirit. Allow Scripture to fill you with a desire to grow in your relationship with the God who dwells within you.

"For in one Spirit we were all baptized into one body—Jews or Greeks, slaves or free—and all were made to drink of one Spirit." 1 Corinthians 12:13

"Or do you not know that your body is a temple of the Holy Spirit within you, whom you have from God? You are not your own." 1 Corinthians 6:19

"And do not get drunk with wine, for that is debauchery, but be filled with the Spirit." Ephesians 5:18

2. Ask the Holy Spirit to fill you afresh today. Ask him to reveal his nearness to you that you might grow in your knowledge of him. Tell him that you want greater relationship with him.

3. Ask the Holy Spirit to empower you to live today free from sin and in total pursuit of God's will being done on the earth through your life. Ask him to give you a clear witness about what it is you should and shouldn't do. Commit yourself to follow his perfect guidance today.

"For all who are led by the Spirit of God are sons of God." Romans 8:14

"But you will receive power when the Holy Spirit has come upon you, and you will be my witnesses in Jerusalem and in all Judea and Samaria, and to the end of the earth." Acts 1:8

No matter where you work, where you live, or what your past is, you can live in total communion with the Holy Spirit. His plans extend far beyond what your job is or which family you're in. He longs to bring the kingdom to earth everywhere you go. He longs to fill you with love and grace for all those around you that you might carry the atmosphere of the kingdom. And he longs to lead you into a continually greater awareness of his love and presence in your life. May your day be marked by joy and fellowship with the Holy Spirit.

Extended Reading: Acts 2

God's Heart to Meet with Man: John on Patmos

DAY 28

DEVOTIONAL

The story of John receiving the book of Revelation from Jesus brings tears to my eyes. I imagine an isolated, weary, and lonely John on Patmos spending his days waiting until he gets to be with his beloved Jesus again. I imagine his heart yearning just to see his friend and Savior. And suddenly, after years of serving Jesus, he appears to John once again, his Lord and King standing before him, speaking to him that which will be the final words of Scripture. In Revelation 1:12-20, John records Jesus coming to meet with him, saying:

"Then I turned to see the voice that was speaking to me, and on turning I saw seven golden lampstands, and in the midst of the lampstands one like a son of man, clothed with a long robe and with a golden sash around his chest. The hairs of his head were white, like white wool, like snow. His eyes were like a flame of fire, his feet were like burnished bronze, refined in a furnace, and his voice was like the roar of many waters. In his right hand he held seven stars, from his mouth came a sharp two-edged sword, and his face was like the sun shining in full strength.

When I saw him, I fell at his feet as though dead. But he laid his right hand on me, saying, "Fear not, I am the first and the last, and the living one. I died, and behold I am alive forevermore, and I have the keys of Death and Hades. Write therefore the things that you have seen, those that are and those that are to take place after this. As for the mystery of the seven stars that you

> "When I saw him, I fell at his feet as though dead. But he laid his right hand on me, saying, 'Fear not, I am the first and the last, and the living one. I died, and behold I am alive forevermore, and I have the keys of Death and Hades. Write therefore the things that you have seen, those that are and those that are to take place after this.'"
>
> **REVELATION 1:17-19**

saw in my right hand, and the seven golden lampstands, the seven stars are the angels of the seven churches, and the seven lampstands are the seven churches."

Imagine the joy and awe in John's heart as his Rabbi Jesus reveals himself in glory to once again share with him history-altering revelation. Imagine the passion John would feel as his last days, which he thought he would spend alone in exile, are interrupted by a final chapter of kingdom work delivered straight from the mouth of his Savior.

God loves to interrupt the seasons of our lives in which we feel most lost with glorious encounters with him. He loves to repurpose us for incredible kingdom work just where we thought we were most useless. He longs to meet with us and envision us for his plans to bring his kingdom to earth. No matter where you are or how old you are, God has tremendous plans in store for all those who will serve him. There is no work he gives us too small. There is no time in our lives that we are unusable. There is no age in which we are to stop being used by our Savior. Jesus longs to meet with you today and tell you of his plans for salvation. He longs to empower you to do a mighty work for his kingdom. He longs for you to see his kingdom come to earth all the days of your life until you take your final breath here and wake up with him. May you receive and share the revelation Jesus gives you today with a world that desperately needs to know him.

GUIDED PRAYER

1. Meditate on God's heart to meet with you in every season of your life. Allow Scripture to fill you with faith and desire to meet with your King today.

"Call to me and I will answer you, and will tell you great and hidden things that you have not known." Jeremiah 33:3

"When the Spirit of truth comes, he will guide you into all the truth, for he will not speak on his own authority, but whatever he hears he will speak, and he will declare to you the things that are to come." John 16:13

"Seek the Lord and his strength; seek his presence continually!" 1 Chronicles 16:11

2. Ask the Holy Spirit to fill you afresh today. Open your heart and receive him that you might live empowered to see the kingdom of God come to earth.

3. Ask God what it is he would have you do today. How does he want to use you to advance his kingdom on the earth?

"Your kingdom come, your will be done, on earth as it is in heaven." Matthew 6:10

What an incredible gift that God would choose to use us for his kingdom purposes. You and I can have a real, eternal impact on the earth. No matter what our age or past failures, God longs to use us. And through the coming of the Holy Spirit, we have God dwelling within us. The same God who raised Christ Jesus from the grave, empowered the disciples for miraculous works, and has been at the root of every great spiritual awakening dwells within us. May you allow God to use you in mighty and powerful ways today to spread the gospel of love everywhere you go.

Extended Reading: Matthew 6